WALKING THROUGH FRANCE

From the Channel to the Camargue

Robin Neillands

ASHFORD, BUCHAN & ENRIGHT
LEATHERHEAD

Published in 1994 by Ashford, Buchan & Enright,
PO Box 20, Leatherhead, Surrey KT24 5HH

First published in 1988

© Robin Hunter Neillands 1988

Maps drawn by Terry Brown

BRITISH LIBRARY CATALOGUING IN PUBLICATION DATA
Hunter, Rob
Walking Through France.
1. –Walking – France 2. France –
Description and travel – 1975
Rn: Robin Hunter Neillands I. Title
914.4'04838   DC29.3

ISBN 1 85253 312 9

Typeset by Priory Publications, Haywards Heath
Printed by FotoDirect Ltd, Brighton

This book is dedicated to Maria,
without whose help I would never
have started, and Geoff Cowen,
without whose help I would never
have finished.

CONTENTS

Acknowledgements 7

One Getting Started 9

Two The Coast to the Suisse-Normande 29

Three South To The Loire 53

Four Along the Indre 77

Five Berri and the Limousin 97

Six Across the Volcano Country 117

Seven Crossing Cantal 137

Eight Margeride, Gévaudan and Aubrac 157

Nine Crossing The Causse Country 175

Ten Cévennes and Garrigue 193

Clothing and Kit List 213

Useful Addresses 214

Select Bibliography 215

Index 216

'When an Englishman has nothing to do, his one recourse is to walk about. A Frenchman sits down and lights a cigar, a German meditates, and an American invents a new position for his limbs, as far as possible asunder from that intended for them by nature . . . but an Englishman always takes a walk.'

Anthony Trollope (1859)

ACKNOWLEDGEMENTS

A great many people have helped me with this journey, so thanks are due to: Geoff Cowen; Henderson MacCartney of McCarta Ltd; Ian Carruthers and Toby Oliver of Brittany Ferries; Odile Herbert of the Normandy Tourist Board; Pauline Hallam and Patrick Goyet of the French Government Tourist Office in London; Shona Crawford Poole of *The Times;* Peter Wright of the *Daily Mail;* Paul and Sarah Howcroft of Rohan Ltd; Beverlie Flower; Derryck Draper of Karrimor; Mlle Renée Payoux of the *Logis de France* organization; the staff of the *Fédération Française pour la Randonnée Pédestre* (FFRP) in Paris; Paul Armandary and the Brittany Ferrets; and Estelle Huxley who kept the home typewriter smoking in my absence.

CHAPTER ONE

GETTING STARTED

'We can all still be travellers, rather than
tourists, if we set our minds to it.'
John Julius Norwich

Two days after I fell off Maria, I decided to walk across France. Maria, he adds hastily, is a horse. At fifty, I was really too old to start riding, but when I was young, during the last war, horses were eaten rather than ridden, and so I came to the matter rather late. Getting on, rising trot and sitting trot all went rather well. But then canter somehow became gallop, and when Maria went left, I continued over her ears onto a rocky hillside in Mallorca. It was two months before I could sit or walk properly again, but at least that painful interval gave me time to think.

I am a travel writer. If you are a travel writer, working at it full time, and for a living rather than for pleasure, then it seems to me that now and again you ought really to travel, push your luck, give it a go, chance your arm, maybe bite off more than you can chew. If this seems a blinding glimpse of the obvious, let me assure you that there are many 'travel writers' who would be unable to grope their way to the end of Southend Pier without a free ticket and a helping hand from the Southend Public Relations person.

I am not that sort of travel writer, but on the other hand, neither am I an explorer nor an adventurer. I'm an ordinary sort of traveller with only a limited amount of spare time, but by gathering up the days over a year or so, I can usually accumulate enough time to attempt something a little out of the ordinary, yet well worth doing. I call these trips my 'adventures on a human scale'. They depend not so much on *where* I travel but *how,* and the most important ingredient seems to be a degree of physical effort and personal commitment. I have – and I mention these journeys only to set the scene for what follows – ridden my bicycle down the Pilgrim Road, from Le Puy to Compostela and, a couple of years later, ridden the Crusader Trail across Turkey and Syria to Jordan and Jerusalem. I have paddled a canoe down the Zambezi, walked south on the Robert Louis Stevenson Trail in France – following his *Travels with a Donkey in the Cévennes,* been on a cattle drive across Montana, and shinned up the occasional mountain. Nothing too strenuous you understand, and all of it possible for anyone with a few weeks to spare. All of it was fun. Then, suddenly, there I was, lying on my back in Mallorca, with a huge assortment of bruises and a chipped vertebra. Well, as I said, it gives a chap time to think.

While I had my feet up, the idea of a walk across France came swimming into my mind and – to mix a metaphor – took root. I had ridden across France by bike and taken a ship for Mallorca on two occasions, so, just to be different, why not walk out from somewhere on the Channel coast, south to the port of Sète on the Mediterranean shore, close to the Camargue? I lay there and looked at the ceiling, feeling the idea grow within my head. Then I made the first of those small moves that lead to irrevocable decisions. Groping to the right, I picked up the telephone and phoned my agent . . . well, after all, I do this for a living and if I was going to do it, I needed to get a book out of it. John listened to the outline, grunted, wished me a swift return to mobility and hung up. I ring John about once a month with some idea or other; some end up as books, some don't. I had almost forgotten about this one, when I met another friend and he said, 'What's this I hear about you walking across France?'

A wise man can always tell when an idea has come home to roost – the moment when you are stuck and have to go through with it. It happens when someone comes up and repeats your thoughts back to you in the form of a commitment. Then follows the fleeting pause, the split second when the loophole is still open and the chance to cop out and say, 'Who? Me?' still exists. Let that moment pass and, for better or worse, you have to go through with it. I have some experience of this. When I was in the Royal Marines, I got very drunk one night with some SBS sergeants and woke up to discover I had volunteered to become a frogman. It took weeks of tearful pleading with my troop commander, who was openly gleeful at my predicament, before I got out of that one. And so it was at this point. I could have said no; as it was, I said yes. The result, more or less, is what follows.

According to the Michelin Guide, the distance from the Channel coast to the Mediterranean is about 600 miles, or 1,000 kilometres. I digested this fact, closed the guide and sat back to look through the window at the autumn rain, shifting uncomfortably in my chair. Having fallen off that horse in Mallorca and eventually regained mobility, I had promptly got back on a horse in Buckinghamshire – and fallen off yet again. Well, if a thing is worth doing, it's worth doing twice. Clearly walking would be more comfortable than riding, at least for the foreseeable future, and immobility is boring. Besides, more and more of my cronies were coming on the phone exclaiming, 'What's this I hear . . . ?' So every day I failed to refute the idea made my departure for the Mediterranean more inevitable. However, since the truth must be told, I didn't really want to do it. We think of distances today in relation to our normal methods of travel, by aircraft, car or train. By any of these, crossing France is a mere bagatelle, but on foot it is different. On foot it's a bloody long way. I have done a lot of walking in France, so I speak of what I know.

In 1978 I had volunteered to organise the Inaugural Walk down what is now the Robert Louis Stevenson Trail, a mere 120 miles from Le Monastier in the Vélay to St-Jean-du-Gard in the Cévennes, following the route taken by RLS and his donkey Modestine on his *Travels with a Donkey in the Cévennes*, a hundred years before. This is now a popular walk, a must in the lifetime of every true walker, a delightful journey with a historic theme, but the inaugural march was different. The weather was hot, the trail ill-defined, our packs heavy. One walker keeled over with heat exhaustion on the first day and lay on his face in the dusty main street of Le Bouchet. Sun-scorched, blistered and exhausted, we crawled into St-Jean-du-Gard at the end of the week, and ten years on, my feet still bear the scars. Since then I have been nineteen miles up and down the Grand Canyon of Colorado, all within a day on the Bright Angel Trail, and been devoured by free-range mosquitoes in the Chilkoot Pass in Alaska on the Trail of the Yukon Gold Rush, plus many other, less exotic foot-powered expeditions. The only abiding memory of them all is that none of them worked out as planned, and all of them were much harder in the execution than they appeared to be at the planning stage. I have become, in short, cautious. If I was going to 'trek off' on my own across France, I would pick the shortest route, take the lightest load, and this time, really enjoy myself.

Though I had blathered myself into that corner of commitment that left me no choice short of shame but to go ahead and do it, I still had a choice of routes. Not being daft, I would choose the shortest route providing a walk from the Channel coast to the Mediterranean, but since this was, after all, a walk, my chosen route must take in the best walking areas along the way, and be undertaken, wherever possible, on footpaths. Here the walker in France has some distinct advantages over the walker in other countries, for France has the well-waymarked footpaths of the *Grande Randonnée.*

We must go back a bit. Britain has the Ramblers' Association, and France has the marvellously entitled *Fédération Française pour la Randonnée Pédestre* (FFRP), and the *Comité National des Sentiers de la Grande Randonnée* (CNSGR). The first is the French equivalent of the Ramblers' Association, and the second, a spin-off from the first, has organised and waymarked a nationwide network of long-distance footpaths or *Grandes Randonnées* or – and any visitor to France must get used to initials – GR. I even had an excuse, a *raison d'être,* to make the effort; the FFRP was established in 1947 and it was now 1987. A trans-France walk on the fortieth anniversary of the FFRP appealed even to the French, who, when they heard about it, were no more than mildly miffed that it should be made by an Englishman. I am, in fact, a Scot, but I have learned not to argue with the French on points of detail. Life is too short.

France has around 30,000 miles of these waymarked, well-established long-distance footpaths, each with its own number, GR1, GR6, GR1O and so on. Many GRs are shown on maps of the *Institut Giographique National* (IGN), and most have their own guidebook or *topo-guide,* giving details of the route, the time required per 'stage' or section, accommodation *en route,* access points by train, history of the places on the way, and so on. All the GR paths are waymarked to a common – or fairly common – system of red and white signs, and many of the paths are equipped with hostels called *gîtes d'étape,* so that, on the face of it, no country in the world is better suited to the long-distance walker. At first glance, all I had to do was buy the appropriate IGN maps and *topo-guides,* pick out a route and proceed gently and gracefully along it from the Channel to the Camargue. Life is never that simple.

Several pages could be devoted to the reasons why it is not possible to alight on the French coast and then simply amble south. Each reason would require a long explanation and tedious amounts of detail, and some of this detail will be revealed in the story which follows, but to put it plainly, here are a few of the snags. Not all the maps show all the footpaths; some of the *topo-guides* are out of print or out of date – French footpaths are being extended all the time and alternative routes or *variantes* often become footpaths in their own right; accurate information on weather, terrain and accommodation proved remarkably hard to come by and, as the wise man said, 'It's better to know nothing than know what ain't so'. There was also the question of time. Since I write for a living the time spent walking and not writing would be unproductive and therefore unprofitable, so clearly there was a limit to the amount of time and effort I could afford to expend. After a good deal of pondering over the calendar, I decided that I could afford a maximum of six weeks. Divided into the distance, that worked out at about fifteen miles – say twenty-four kilometres – a day . . . every day. This seemed a moderate target, and I am at one in this with Dr Baedeker, who wrote back in 1899 that 'The walker's (daily) performances should be moderate; and even when he is in good training, they should rarely exceed ten hours' walking a day.'

Time and distance decided, there came next the questions of where to walk and how. These two are linked by the accommodation factor. Should I go all out and backpack, carrying the complete wherewithal for self-sufficiency in my rucksack and so avoid hotels? Or should I plot a route which ensured a good bed, a hot meal and a shower at the end of the day? Long backpacking trips mean heavy loads, and a one-week training walk across the Pyrenees convinced me that lugging a forty-five-pound (twenty-kilo) pack over mountains at my age was less than pleasant. I soon decided that this should be an enjoyable ramble, not a backpacking expedition, but here again there were problems. Not every little village has a hotel, and not every hotel would be open when I passed by. I could become benighted in the mountains or lost in the fog. I put a big red circle around 'accommodation' on my list of queries and decided that I would have to take a tent and a sleeping bag for the odd occasion when I might get stuck; anyway I would need the bag for the *gîtes d'étape*. Whenever possible, though, I would stay in hotels, preferably in the small country hotels of the *Logis de France* network, places where the owners are always friendly and have no strong objection to muddy boots in the bar.

This is how the planning stage works. Ideas are suggested or come drifting into your mind: the good ones stay and are adopted, the bad ones fall by the wayside, those in the middle get adapted and put to use in a slightly different form. I'm not too committed to the idea of a firm step-by-step plan. I think there should be room for error and experiment, for the possibility that things might well – and indeed should – go wrong. Paul Theroux is on record as saying that, 'Travel writing is a funny thing because the worst trips make the best reading', and I agree with him. This thought in turn led me to the Brittany Ferrets . . . they like it when things go wrong.

Some ten years ago, I wrote a book about Brittany. When it was finished and on the point of publication, it had to be promoted, for there are, after all, many books about Brittany. I therefore suggested to the shipping line, Brittany Ferries, that I should organise a walk on a *Grande Randonnée*, and that they should invite some Press people to come on it, thereby seeing parts of Brittany as yet unknown to the more cosseted traveller. Four of us – Peter Chambers, Don Philpott, John Lloyd, and I – went on the first Brittany Ferry Walk, a four-day jaunt up the GR38 from Rennes to Mont-St-Michel. Such was its success that the walk has since become an annual event based on one or other of the Brittany Ferry destinations and organised, or to be more accurate, cobbled together, by the Brittany Ferries Press and Public Relations man, Toby Oliver, and me. These trips are attended by a steadfast group of regulars collectively known as the Brittany Ferrets: Deborah Penn, Alison Bruce, John Lloyd, Peter Chambers, Keith Howells, Paul Armandary, and Carol Matheson. The only requirements are that everyone should have a good time, that lots of Press articles shall follow, and that – something should go wrong. It was also relevant that the Brittany Ferrets can walk. Sixty miles in four days is not for everyone. The rule about things going wrong seemed particularly relevant to my purpose, so I picked up the phone and suggested to Toby that my walk across France should be accompanied, for four days at least, by a team from the Brittany Ferrets.

'I thought you'd never ask,' he said. 'Where do we go from, and when?'

Good point. There are no less than nine Channel ports giving access to the French countryside: Dunkerque, Calais, Boulogne, Dieppe, Le Hâvre, Ouistreham, Cherbourg, St Malo and Roscoff. Which should I choose as a starting point? Bearing in mind that I wanted to cover the shortest distance in a limited amount of time, the process of elimination was fairly simple. Dunkerque gives out onto the dreary Flanders plain, while Calais and Boulogne offer endless miles across Artois and Picardy before any interesting country comes along. The same is true of Dieppe and Le Hâvre, and with all of these departure points the walker heading south has to cope with a long haul round Paris. This leaves the Norman and Breton ports. Since Roscoff, out near Finistère, is too far away, and Cherbourg would add the Cotentin Peninsula to the distance, that left Ouistreham or St Malo. I had already ridden on my bicycle from St Malo to the Mediterranean, so the final choice came down to Ouistreham at the northern end of the Caen Canal.

This had, in addition, some other advantages. It was – with the possible exception of St Malo – the shortest route I could choose. The GR36 footpath actually begins on the Channel coast beside the ferry port and I could follow it south, at least to the Loire. Ouistreham is a newly opened ferry port, without the likelihood that some other walker had been this way before, and the area round about has historic links with Britain, dating back to William the Conqueror and, more recently, to D-Day. As to choosing my final destination, I simply laid a ruler across the map and drew a direct line to the Mediterranean, since the shortest distance between any two points is said to be a straight line – though not necessarily on foot. Direct routes are popular with climbers who, when all other routes to the summit have been climbed, assault the mountain on a line that a drop of water might follow from the top. A *direttissima* across France is not possible, but I stuck as close to that pencilled route as possible and it ran into the sea at Palavas-les-Flots, south of Montpellier. Toby and I therefore decided that our annual Brittany Ferry Walk would begin at Ouistreham and follow my route south across the Suisse-Normande. For this first section, Ouistreham to Putanges-Pont-Ecrepin, we allowed four days.

Departure time was another consideration. Aiming for a publication date in late spring, I needed to leave England as soon as possible in the spring of the preceding year. This appealed to me because the weather promised to be cool. I had learnt all about the dire effects of heat when on the Robert Louis Stevenson Trail and when riding my bike to Compostela. Hot weather and hard walking are not compatible. Like most walkers, I like cool, even cold, crisp days, when the views are vast and the skies clear, rather than those hot, enervating days of summer which quickly drain strength and blister feet. The route from Ouistreham would give me the chance to get fit before the days warmed up and the terrain turned mountainous. This was yet another reason for walking south, rather than flying down to the Mediterranean and walking back to England – another of the many suggestions that were falling on me thick and fast as the plan began to crystalise into a firm project. Besides, as we all know, walking south is downhill. Even so, given all the alternatives there remained plenty of possible snags. Winter hangs on late, until well into April or May on the mountains of the Massif Central, and northern springs are not always green and pleasant. However, there is not much one can do about the weather except pray, and a spring departure provided the best possible option.

All this extra work and thought had to be fitted into the normal writing day – if a freelance writer ever has a normal writing day and when I had covered every spare scrap of paper with scribbled notes and lists, I thought the time had come to state my aims succinctly on a single sheet of paper, and so clear my head. The outline went something like this:

I would walk south across France in the spring, from the port of Ouistreham on the Channel coast, north of Caen, to Palavas, west of the Camargue delta on the Mediterranean, a distance of about 700 miles (1,127 kilometres). I would travel on the footpaths of the *Grande Randonnée* whenever possible. I would stay in hotels but take some supporting equipment, just in case I got stuck. I could allow no more than six weeks for the journey as, leaving on 25 March, I must be back by 9 May, the fourteenth birthday of my daughter, Claire. (Those who think this last a trivial reason don't know my daughter Claire.) I did not wish to walk more than twenty miles a day and I wanted to direct my route through some of the best walking areas of France. Most of all, it must be fun.

Set out like this, and taking up less than half a sheet of paper, it looked easy. However, relating it to the maps, the varied terrain, the time of year, the accommodation and the amount of equipment necessary to execute the plan and record this event for posterity, the project seemed more of a challenge than I was really prepared for. I gathered up this statement and all the material and went to have lunch with Toby.

'What you need now,' he said, 'is a plan – a detailed plan.'

'This is the plan.'

'That's not a plan,' said Toby, firmly. 'That's a declaration of intent. You need a day-by-day, step-by-step plan, where to, how far, which way . . . the lot. Make a plan, old son, that's my advice.' Planning is not my forte. I much prefer to play it by ear. Besides, planning is time-consuming and I was very busy. On the other hand, it *is* a very long way on foot from the Channel to the Mediterranean, so perhaps Toby was right. I thought of the best planner I know, and rang Geoff Cowen.

Geoff is a planner, an organiser, a man who knows his own mind. My office is a shambles, and my main dread is that someone will get into it and tidy up. Geoff's office is a study in symmetry. I keep notes on cigarette packets and torn paper napkins; Geoff makes lists in ruled notebooks. Had Geoff planned the D-Day invasion of Normandy, the last war would have ended in 1943. That apart, he's a friend of mine – and he likes to walk. We used to be partners in a publishing business which, in spite of all our efforts, refused to make a profit, and if you can survive that and still be on speaking terms, it speaks well for your relationship. If anyone could work out a detailed programme for my walk across France it would be Geoff. I bundled all my maps *and topo-guides* into the car and drove round to see him.

'I like your assumption that I've got damn-all else to do than plan this for you,' said Geoff. 'And I don't wish to be critical or anything, but don't you think you're getting a bit old for all this?' He may have had a point there, but I didn't think so. After all, John Hillaby was a year older when he set out on his journey through Britain from Land's End to John O'Groats, and he has put in some impressive mileages in the years since. If I had a sensible, detailed plan, one which I could stick to with only the minimal amount of effort, I could see no real difficulty. But then, I'm like that; Geoff is the one to spot the snags.

Just for a start, he pointed out, it is a very long way from the Channel coast to the Mediterranean and I wanted to do it in six weeks or less. According to Geoff, that meant walking about twenty miles a day, every day, which would swiftly introduce an attrition factor. Walking twenty miles a day is not too much, but twenty miles a day, day after day, across all kinds of terrain and in whatever degree of awfulness the weather patterns could provide, was something else again. There was going to be the need for a day off now and again, to rest the feet and wash the socks, but at least as time went by, I would get fitter.

Geoff is very hot on the subject of fitness, and keeps himself in some sort of trim with his once- or twice-weekly sessions on the rugby pitch. Now that's very wise, but I have a decided aversion to fitness. If I find the urge to exercise coming on, I lie down hurriedly and press the sofa until the mood passes off. This is not to say that getting fit – or at least fitter – before setting off to walk across France was not a thoroughly good idea. Indeed, if anyone else was going to do it, I would regard it as essential. But getting fit is both time-consuming and boring. Over the years I have tried various short-cuts back to a younger, fitter me; the garage is cluttered with rusting exercise bicycles and hardly used rowing machines. I tried jogging for a while, and gave it up gleefully when I read that it can cause heart attacks.

This explanation cut little ice with Geoff, who made me promise that I would try to get a little fitter before the start, before he finally agreed to take over all the maps and guides and plan out a detailed route, on footpaths, stage by daily stage, all the way from Ouistreham to the Camargue. But on one condition.

'And what's that?'

'That I can come with you – for at least part of the way.'

'It's a deal,' I said.

The American writer, Paul Fussell, has commented that '. . . he travels fastest who travels alone but he who travels best, travels with a companion.' Companions can be a problem on any long-distance venture, which is one of the reasons why I usually prefer either to go alone or team up with someone I meet along the way. This is not because friends or companions are unwelcome, but because, when we get right down to it, their ideas of what should happen *en route* rarely coincide with mine and friction eventually develops. I'm not alone in this; many a well-found expedition has disintegrated because the members fell out or simply got on each other's nerves. Besides, if I was going to walk across France, my favourite country, I wanted to do it on my own and not be leader for a pack. But there are exceptions to every rule, notably the Ferrets and Geoff, who are people I can get along with even in adversity, even when things go wrong. In fact, we fix it so they do.

On previous Brittany Walks we have slogged across Finistère in driving rain and wind, slept in assorted hell-holes and chilly caves beside the Loire, and, most memorably, trudged across the snow-girt mountains of the Picos de Europa in northern Spain to the little village of Sotres, the manure capital of Europe. Ten minutes after we marched in, we renamed it Sotres-sur-Merde. The main occupation of this village is shifting large amounts of cow-dung from one end of the village to the other by mule train and, as we sat in a grimy bar, with liquid slurry washing about our boots, Toby confided, 'I didn't think people in Europe lived like this any more.' There was no doubt that the Ferrets could hack it across Normandy and have fun, and Geoff, a keen rugby coach, was both fit and a good companion. Besides, there is a limit to the amount of self-revelation any book should contain. My own company might pall a bit after a few weeks – at the time and even on paper afterwards – so such good companions were welcome. Even so, I wanted others along only for part of the trip – the bulk of it I wanted to keep to myself. That settled, while Toby rounded up fit Ferrets and Geoff pored over the maps, I went to round up the kit.

Long-distance walkers have a problem with kit: weight. It is possible to take all you need to sustain yourself over moor and mountain for weeks on end, but only if you are prepared to hump a considerable burden, the weight of which will press your feet flat by the end of every day. Should the terrain permit, it is equally possible to stroll from hotel to hotel with your hands in your pockets, if some kind soul will transport your suitcase ahead each day. My problem lay somewhere between the two extremes. On the one hand, I had no wish to undertake an all-out beard-and-muesli-style backpacking trip. On the other hand, if I was to stay on the GR footpaths and walk across the wilder parts of the Auvergne, the Gévaudan and the Cévennes – remote areas at any time, and tricky in the early spring when the weather, to say the least, can be changeable and, when rough, very rough indeed – it would be only sensible to take some essential wherewithal to keep body and soul together should I get stuck on a hill, alone, with night descending. I decided to gather up everything I needed, cram it all into the rucksack and weigh it. The scale quivered to a halt at forty-six pounds. Hmmn!

Out came the spare boots, the ice-axe and all the freeze-dried food. Weight now thirty-eight pounds – still not good enough. Out came the second set of spare clothing, reducing my wardrobe from one on, one off and one in the wash, to a maximum of one on, one off; out came the SVEA petrol stove and the cook-set – I'd eat cold food if necessary. Weight now: thirty-two pounds – better. I kept this up until, stripped down to the barest essentials, the pack weighed twenty-seven pounds. This felt fairly light – and then I remembered that Geoff had the maps and *topo-guides,* and I had still to add two cameras, spare film (and lots of it), notebooks, a recording machine – oh Lord! The final all-up weight when I staggered off the Brittany Ferry was thirty-five pounds. Therefore I had decided to devote a certain amount of time and ingenuity to persuading someone to transport the rucksack south whenever possible. Low, rat-like cunning is said to be part of every journalist's equipment.

The maps and *topo-guides* pack alone weighed around five pounds. According to the pundits, I should either have purchased suitable topographic maps as I went along or sent them ahead, *poste-restante* for collection *en route*. But having had some little experience myself, I decided to assemble everything I needed at the start and to put up with the weight, for it is axiomatic that the one map which local shops have always sold out of is the local one and, while *poste-restante* may work, I did not know if the little villages I would pass through even had a post office, or if it would be open during my visit. Neither could I wait nor divert to the main post office in the nearest big town – winged time was always at my heels.

One way of compensating for the luggage restriction is to take the best you can find – which is usually the lightest anyway. I decided to take two sets of Rohan clothing, one on, one off, because Rohan is both windproof and presentable, because it washes easily, dries quickly, packs small and weighs very little. Best of all, the pockets have zips. I packed my now ancient Black's 'Icelandic' sleeping bag, faded and stained from many a trip, but warm and light. I took a Bob Saunders 'Jet-Packer' tent and a Thermarest mattress and a Silva compass, and as many pairs of loop-stitched socks as I could cram into the corners of the rucksack. With the green beret given to me by my ex-Commando cronies as a reminder that we had all been good kids once, my personal equipment was almost complete. Those of a technical bent will find a complete kit list in the appendix.

Equipment assembled, and the result crammed into my Karrimor 'Jaguar' rucksack, I turned the focus on my feet. No one contemplating even a weekend walk can afford to ignore his feet, and nothing would bring my expedition to a swifter stop than a bad dose of blisters – the Robert Louis Stevenson Trail had taught me that. Loop-stitched socks may be half the battle, but the real weapon is a well-broken-in pair of comfortable walking boots.

I had a pair of boots which I wore continuously during the months before departure. Then, just two weeks before leaving, I decided not to take them. I really needed a half size and boots don't always come in half sizes. My broken-in pair were very comfortable and had given no hint of blistering but, when going downhill, my toes bumped hard into the ends. That might be acceptable on a day or a weekend walk, but not for more than six hundred miles. Like most walkers, I often find going downhill even more tiring than going uphill, and it is certainly a greater strain on the legs. I spent most of one Saturday afternoon irritating the staff of the local outdoor shop by trying on their entire stock of boots and eventually emerged with a state-of-the-art pair of Daisy Roots, light, flexible boots with (to quote the product publicity) 'a Scatola system having whole cut uppers, in a tough resilient leather with a carefully shaped, padded tongue and collar, and a calf lining; plus cleated Mukluk soles with integral heel-grip, plus a new nylon Graduflex system insole and an Anatomic footbed'. Space-age stuff indeed.

Boot fashions change every few years among the walking fraternity. Big, heavy clumpers alternate in popularity with light boots or even trainers. Currently, light, flexible boots are all the rage but I have often noted that long-distance walkers, whatever boots they start out in, seem to switch to light ones in the end. Worn with a frequently changed pair of loop-stitched socks, my Daisy Roots took me across France without a single blister, although the 'cleated Mukluk soles' wore flat long before the end of the walk.

A month before the 'off', I was as ready for the trip as I ever would be – except that, as always, I was unfit. I had been halfway out of the door many a time, fully loaded, and all set for an hour or so trolling round the local lanes, when the telephone rang and hauled me back to my desk. I managed to fit in a few ten- or twelve-mile walks in the month before the start, but I was still out of shape when the day of departure finally arrived. Otherwise matters were proceeding well. I now had Geoff's route, on which he had laboured for weeks before bringing it round one evening to discuss it with me.

'Now, let us just outline, once again, what you are after,' he said, spreading drifts of maps and guides across the carpet. 'You want to walk from the Channel to the Med, in as direct a route as possible between, say, Caen and Sète, using the GR footpaths, staying in hotels or *gîtes*, boozing every evening, and getting back in six weeks – right?'

'Correct.'

'Well, if – and it's a big if – you follow this route, make every daily stage, and don't get tired, blistered or hung-over, you can do this route . . .' Geoff tapped the map, ' . . . in about six weeks. That's at an average of just over seventeen miles a day, less at the start across Normandy when we go with the gang, more as you get fitter. I've even allowed for two days off, one here in Tours on the Loire, and another here at St Flour after you have crossed the Auvergne. It still comes to 700 miles, not the 600 you were hoping for – 714 to be exact.'

Clearly a great deal of thought and study had gone into Geoff's plan, and he had managed to fit all the necessary elements into the time without exhausting the main contender. His route began beside the ferry link-span in Ouistreham, and followed the GR36 south across Normandy and the Sarthe to the Loire Valley, leading across two great walking areas of northern France: the hills of the Suisse-Normande country along the River Orne, and the vast Parc Normandie-Maine which straddles the frontier of Normandy and the Sarthe.

Pressing on to cross the Rivers Loire and Cher at Tours – 'We can slope off here for the day and look at the chateaux,' said Geoff – the route followed the newly opened GR46 which still had no *topo-guide* and was shown only on the newer maps. 'So let's hope it's waymarked.' The GR46 ran all the way east, down the Indre Valley to Châteauroux, where I would switch to follow the GR41 across the top corner of the Limousin, through La Châtre to Boussac and Evaux-les-Bains, into the Auvergne, and onto the GR4 (Section Aubusson to St Flour) in the north of the Puy-de-Dôme.

'There's another big problem here,' said Geoff. 'The *topo-guide* we need, GR4 (Aubusson to St Flour), is out of print. I couldn't get a copy for love nor money, so I can't plot the route precisely or fix stops. You'll have to try and find one when you get down there. If the weather is bad, this might be the worst part of the route. Since the Ferrets peel off at Putanges, south of the Suisse-Normande, and I go home at Tours, you'll be on your own there.' From Evaux-les-Bains the route headed south across the Puy-de-Dôme into the volcano country of the Massif Central, between Orcival and Le Mont-Dore. 'You said you wanted to see the church in Orcival, so I've put that in, but after that, God knows how you'll get across the Puy de Sancy above Le Mont-Dore – it's sure to be snow-covered when you get there, and there is no road. Anyway, that's your problem.' The route then went south to the next main range, the Monts du Cantal above the ski resort of Super-Lioran, where the GR4 climbs the Plomb du Cantal which, at 6,086 feet was almost as high as the Puy de Sancy. 'You *said* you wanted problems, so that's another one for you,' Geoff pointed out. 'Don't come crying to me if it goes wrong up there.'

After the Plomb the GR4 turned east across open country to the hill-top fortress city of St Flour, where Geoff's route turned south, following two regional GRs: the *GR du Pays* – the *Sentier du Haute Auvergne* to St-Juéry – and the *Sentier des Monts de l'Aubrac,* south to Aumont-Aubrac. The last footpath, the GR60, the *Grande Draille du Languedoc,* would take me across the Gévaudan and the Tarn Gorges via the Grandes Causses, then up Mont Aigoual and through the wild Cévennes into the *garrigue* country by St-Martin-de-Londres, and so, at last, to the Mediterranean.

The maps stretched out across the carpet from one end of the room to the other.

'The GR60 actually ends here,' said Geoff, tapping the last map. 'At Tréviers, about ten miles east of St-Martin-de-Londres. I can't think why. Once you get there it's only about twenty-five miles to the Med. You can work that part out for yourself. Well, that's the bulk of it. What do you think?'

I thought it was terrific. Working out a long route is never easy, because the pieces just don't fit. A pleasant, twenty-mile stage leaves you at dusk in the middle of nowhere. Stop at an hotel five miles earlier and you have an extra five miles to do next day; go on five miles to the next one, and you finish the day drained, with it all to do again on the morrow. Geoff had worked and reworked the route to make the pieces fit, and the result looked both interesting and possible.

'I'll give it a go,' I said. 'Let's show it to the Ferrets.'

The Ferrets also thought it terrific, not least because every stage for the first four days led to a pleasant restaurant in time for lunch, and a small hotel in time for a shower, dinner, and an hour or two putting the world to rights around the bar before bed. Only after Putanges-Pont-Ecrepin did the stages lengthen, and with the departure of the Press support team in their cars, our heavy rucksacks would finally have to be humped. But by then, with luck, I would be fit.

'Tell me,' asked Peter Chambers, 'has anyone ever done this before – walked across France from the Channel to the Med?'

'Not so far as I know,' I said. 'At least, if they have, they haven't written a book about it. I believe an escaped prisoner of war walked to the Pyrenees in 1943 and, in the Middle Ages, Crusaders must have marched south to embark at Aigues-Mortes, but no modern walkers seem to have done it. Someone must have, of course, but until someone else does, I'll claim it as a first.'

'Er . . . one thing . . . Are you going to cheat?' asked John Lloyd.

That was, and still is, a regular question, so to clear the air, I'll confirm that no, I didn't cheat. In fact, the opportunity to hitch a lift happened only once, when a tractor stopped beside me at ten in the morning; feeling fresh I was able to decline. Had a similar temptation occurred at six in the evening, when I was crawling along in a daze after twenty miles or more – who knows? Most of the time, I was far away from any transport, and at other times, the large, lone, wet, be-rucksacked walker is not the ideal passenger to pickup on a lonely country road.

The day of departure coincided with the annual French Government Tourist Office Workshop at the Agricultural Hall in North London, where all the various regions and *départements* of France come to display their attractions to the British tourist trade. This provided what is now known as a photographic opportunity, so fully loaded and wearing my walking boots and clothing, I strode about the carpark, posing for the Press in wildest Islington, before striding off round the corner and, once out of sight, climbing into the front seat of Toby Oliver's Mercedes.

'Where now?' he asked.

'Take me to France,' I said. 'And be quick about it – before I change my mind.'

CHAPTER TWO

THE COAST TO THE SUISSE-NORMANDE

'Let the tourist be cushioned against misadventure.
The true traveller has not had his money's worth
unless he brings back a few scars.'
Lawrence Durrell

I should not have been too surprised that several things went wrong before we even started. The first problem was a murrain among the volunteer walkers. Since even this first phase from the coast to Putanges involved a fairly serious trek of fifteen miles a day or more across hills, we had decided to exclude those Ferrets who might wilt without a daily cosseting in fluffy pink towels. Instead we recruited some serious walkers from the host of volunteers who had, at some stage, expressed the wish to join me in walking across France. My experience is that one actual walker per ten volunteers is about the normal ratio, as people's enthusiasm for a bit of physical effort declines as the time approaches when they may have to make it. Apart from this accepted rate of fall-out though, our more stalwart volunteers became accident-prone. Alan Franks of *The Times,* who is a self-confessed walkaholic, dropped out because, on an assignment to the South Atlantic, he had managed to leave his walking boots under a bed at The Upland Goose in the Falkland Islands, an excuse so unlikely that it had to be true. Peter declared that he always covered himself against such a disaster by

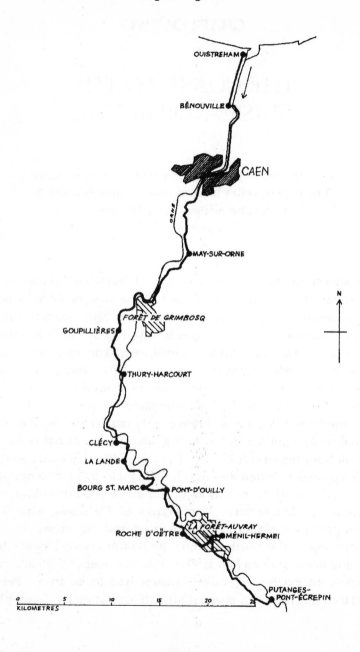

having two pairs of walking boots, but we reminded him of the time when he had brought two left boots with him on a previous trip. Then Geoff, the brains behind the whole operation, rang to say that while playing rugby the previous week, someone had stamped hard on his toes.

'So . . . ?'

'The snag is I can't get my boots on – but don't worry, I'll be there on the night.'

On the night, as the Ferrets assembled at the Portsmouth ferry port, Geoff wasn't there. Instead, we had a message, and a pale, wan voice on the telephone, full of excuses. Something had disagreed with Geoff over lunch that day, and he was currently light green and sick a-bed. We told him to join us when he could, and embarked on the *Duc de Normandie*, for France.

'Don't you feel,' said Toby, as we took up our stations in the bar, 'that this little caper of yours has a jinx on it? Two people have gone down already, and we are still tied up to the dock.' 'It can only get worse,' said John, hopefully. 'Look on the bright side.'

On that happy note, we sailed.

No matter how many times I do it – and I must have crossed the Channel a hundred times or more – there is always a little frisson of excitement as the ship puts out to sea. This is particularly true at Portsmouth, where the ferry glides past lines of grey warships, past the dockyard where HMS *Victory* lies becalmed for all time, past the Solent forts and the Nab Tower, built to defend this great naval base from seaward attack, and so out to sea. There is a great deal of history in this narrow stretch of water. Henry V set sail from here to invade France in 1415, and it was from here in 1944 that the D-Day invasion forces set out, like us, for the shores of Normandy.

Ouistreham, our present destination, lies at the northern end of the Caen Canal and, in 1944, Ouistreham marked the eastern end of the seaborne landings at Sword beach, one of five beaches around the bay of the Seine between the Cotentin peninsula and the Orne, where the Allied forces landed on the dawn of D-Day. Further east, across the Orne and the Caen Canal, the British Sixth Airborne Division had landed earlier in the night to secure the bridges, overrun the great Merville battery, and capture the heights around Ranville from which the defending German forces could otherwise have enfiladed the landing beaches and the offshore shipping. It all looks peaceful enough today, especially on a bright spring morning, but it wasn't always like this hereabouts.

Before sailing, I had asked an old friend of mine, Brigadier Peter Young, about the D-Day landings.

'I took 3 Commando ashore at La Brèche – it lies just up the beach from Ouistreham, and getting ashore was quite a sticky affair. The sea was rough and we lost about thirty men from machine-gun fire just crossing the beach . . . the Germans didn't want us there, you know. Then we linked up with 4 and 45 Commando and marched like hell to join the Parachute Division across the Orne, crossing the bridge at Bénouville just two minutes late . . . you'll see all that on your walk, but I doubt if you'll get such a warm reception as we did, back in '44.'

One advantage of a night crossing is that you usually get some sleep, and an early start in the morning. In this case, rather too early – 6.30 a.m. our time, albeit one hour later in France. We had breakfast on the bridge with the Captain and his officers, a rather silent affair, then descended the gangplank into a bright, clear, cold day. We were met by a lone reporter from the local Press, Odile Herbert from the Normandy Tourist Office, and our French Ferret, Paul Armandary, who had been on several previous expeditions and knew full well that on our trips few things go as planned. Odile, however, was in a high state of nerves.

'I am so anxious that nothing should go wrong,' she said. 'I want you to enjoy your passage through Calvados.'

We assured her that we liked it if things went wrong and that anyway, with two members missing, her hopes had already been dashed. Then the rest withdrew to a discreet distance while I tramped up and down the quay before the lone cameraman from *France-Ouest*. Since I had spent the previous half-hour rehearsing throw-away replies which mingled modesty with tenacity, this small turnout was a disappointment.

'I thought you told me that the local Press would be here in droves,' I hissed at Toby, setting my face in a determined grin and setting out across France for the tenth time. 'Where the hell are they?'

'They'll be here,' said Toby, soothingly. 'You'll be famous before the day is out – I promise.'

If, as Andy Warhol said, everyone can be famous for fifteen minutes, fifteen minutes is probably quite enough for any normal person. The local Press were late, but a camera crew from the France-3 network ambushed us a mile down the canal, skidding their car to a halt alongside, with a request that I go back to the beginning and start again. I had already become very reluctant to walk an extra step in any direction but south, but they got round that objection by offering me a lift back, opening the car door invitingly. Cameras instantly leapt into the hands of the Ferrets.

'Look at that!' said John loudly, snapping away. 'Only a mile into the walk and already he's accepting a lift.'

Just for the record, the camera crew made me walk all the way back to their pick-up point. During the rest of the day we met reporters and photographers all over the place; on street corners, in bars, over lunch at our midday halt and, on one occasion, in the gents' lavatory. By mid-afternoon I was into dark glasses and anxious for a beard.

The GR36 is one of the longest footpaths on the *Grande Randonnée*, running from the Channel at Ouistreham, all the way south to the distant Pyrenees, right through the heartland of France. Apart from the main artery itself, this footpath, like all the other GR trails, is well equipped with alternative routes or *variantes* and, if followed precisely, the GR36 takes well over 250 miles just to get to the Loire. I was leafing through the GR36 *topo-guide*, wondering where we could trim some distance from this route, when I made the interesting discovery that my copy had ten crucial pages missing. As the Ferrets were already starting to straggle, I decided to keep this news to myself. The day was clear and sunny, the footpath nice and flat, and our rucksacks in Odile's car – so far, so good.

Ouistreham is a good place to begin a walk across France, because the GR36 takes the walker directly into a region of great historic interest. On D-Day, the link between the airborne and seaborne forces astride the Orne and the Caen Canal depended on two bridges over the river and canal at Bénouville. The bridges – and in particular what is now Pegasus Bridge over the canal – was taken by *coup-de-main* on the night of 5-6 June. A glider force of the Oxford and Buckinghamshire Light Infantry crash-landed their gliders on the banks of the canal and overwhelmed the defenders before they had time to detonate charges and destroy the bridges. Today, Ouistreham is a pleasant little resort, a grey and white collection of houses which had slumbered peacefully since Norman times until the D-Day forces swept ashore in 1944. The town fell quite quickly and without excessive damage, so that apart from a small museum dedicated to the French troops of No. 4 Commando, and one or two crumbling concrete blockhouses, there are few signs of war. The Caen Canal, which runs for six miles inland to the city, was built in the last century, and turned Caen into a major port, although small coastal craft had made their way up the Orne to Caen since medieval times. Now quite large sea-going vessels can berth at the old ducal capital, and a big container ship cruised past as we marched up the tow-path to Bénouville and Pegasus Bridge.

Apart from the odd hole torn in the ironwork by a shell splinter, and a small artillery piece in a concrete emplacement at one end, Pegasus Bridge looks much like any other cantilevered swing-bridge, but one made strangely familiar from the old wartime photos. Various signboards and plaques set about the site record the events of 6 June 1944, and a sign above the door of the nearby bar announces the fact that this was the first house in France to be liberated by the Allied forces on D-Day. The Ferrets felt that choosing a bar as the first place to liberate seemed to show the right kind of spirit. Across the canal, a Centaur tank of the Royal Marines Armoured Support Regiment rusts away quietly on its plinth, while a scattered group of obelisks now marks the spots where Major John Howard's gliders landed on that momentous night so many years ago. The liberated bar, Chez Goudrée, was closed, but Chez Jo was open, so we slunk in there for our first pit-stop. Begin as you mean to go on, is one of the Ferret mottoes.

Exploring the relics around Pegasus Bridge and capering about for French television camera crews put us in the mood for lunch, and this might be the time to point out that there will be a great deal of eating and drinking in this book, as is only proper in a book about France, where eating and drinking is a serious business. Among my initial instructions to Geoff, who was now languishing on dry biscuits and Malvern water back in Britain, had been one which required him to ensure that at least one decent hotel or restaurant lay across our path each day. The first few days of our walk lay in the hands of Paul Armandary who, being half-French and under stern instructions from the Ferrets, had laid on not one good watering-hole a day but two, beginning with the Hôtel Espérance at Hérouville-St-Clair, just beside the canal, which we reached after three hours on the trail and with seven miles completed – only 693 miles to go. Our pace quickened as we side-stepped the waiting arms of a man from Radio Caen and surged up the steps, past the notice-board promising *Fruits de mer . . . poissons . . . spécialités régionales, cuisine soignée.* . . . As I have said, no one comes between the Ferrets and good French food.

The snag with cities today is that they all have too much suburb. The walker enters the outskirts, passes the sign which marks the city limits and thinks he has arrived – an hour later he is still arriving. So it is with most cities and so it is with Caen, the capital of Lower Normandy, a fine city but one which has long since outgrown its medieval walls. Caen was the capital of the Norman dukes in the years before the Conquest of England and, although well over half the city was totally destroyed in the 1944 Battle of Normandy, a surprising number of ancient buildings remain, carefully restored to their former state where they had suffered war damage. The two great abbeys of Caen – William the Conqueror's Abbaye aux Hommes and his wife Matilda's Abbaye aux Dames – were built by the Duke and his Duchess as an act of penance and to lift the excommunication placed on them by the Pope for marrying within the limits of consanguinity; they were cousins. William was buried in his abbey but his bones were exhumed and thrown into the River Orne during the Revolution. However, according to Odile, enough of his bones have recently been found to enable the abbey to re-inter the Duke in the not too distant future.

The Normans, of course, were the Norsemen, the Vikings. They came sweeping south across the wild North Sea in their narrow ships, forging up any river wide enough for oars, and in the space of a century they had thrown Western Christendom into turmoil. 'If there were a hundred tongues in every head,' wrote an Irish monk at the time, 'they could not recount or retell or renumerate all we have suffered at the hands of that valiant, wrathful, purely pagan people'.

In 911 AD, Charles the Simple, King of the French, bought off Rollo the Viking by the Treaty of St Claire-sur-Epte, ceding him the territory that is now Normandy, and after that the 'Normans', while no less rapacious, abandoned mere raiding for permanent conquest. The Hautevilles established their dukedom at Apulia in Italy, Duke William, the seventh in the line, left his capital at Caen to overcome the kingdom of the Saxons, and Norman knights threw the Empire of Byzantium into turmoil. Most of the warriors who scaled the walls of Jerusalem at the end of the First Crusade in 1099 could trace their line back to some Viking freebooter. Then, quite suddenly, they were gone, their urgency and vigour extinguished. It's very curious that the storm that had swept across the western world for over two hundred years should blow itself out in less than a single generation, but that is what happened.

Caen is much more than a Norman city. It has a history that spans a full millenium, and one which contains many links with the English. John, Duke of Bedford, brother of Henry V, founded the university there in 1437, and English Kings, Angevin and Plantagenet, held the city on and off until as late as 1450. It is also worth remembering that our present Queen holds the Channel Islands – the last relic of our French possessions, which the French still call the *Iles Anglo-Normandes* – by her right as Duke of Normandy. That apart, Caen is a very fair city with a fine castle which is well worth inspecting, but the Ferrets were keen to press on.

We passed by the Abbaye aux Dames, skirted the dock at the Bassin-St-Pierre and the Ducal castle, much restored after heavy shelling in 1944, and limped past the racecourse at La Prairie. Following the waymarks south to St-André-sur-Orne, we pulled ourselves wearily into May-sur-Orne, urged uphill by strong gusts of wind and capfuls of rain. Part of this long afternoon's walk was down the track of the Suisse-Normande railway, a route which, though flat, found no favour with Peter, who had developed a noticeable limp.

'Something has gone seriously wrong with my feet,' he said through clenched teeth. 'The famous loop-stitched socks do not appear to be functioning too well. No, I won't look – not yet – let's get to the hotel, and soon.'

The route from Ouistreham up the Caen Canal, through the city and south to the little town of May at the top of the Suisse-Normande, gave us a stage of about eighteen miles, rather a long and weary stretch for the first day, and it was after seven before we trailed round the church at May and up to our first night stop at the Hôtel l'Ammonite. Here we were warmly welcomed by Madame Horel, who had seen us all on the midday television news, and was suitably impressed, presenting us to the regulars in the bar as her visiting celebrities. This is not necessarily flattering, for a celebrity, in my limited experience, is someone who, while shaking your hand, keeps his or her eyes fixed over your shoulder in case someone more interesting or useful should come into the room. Fortunately, the regulars here, like all true Normans, were underawed and greeted us with a solid row of backs.

There are many good things to say about the Hôtel l'Ammonite: the warm welcome, the eventually friendly bar, the good food, and the billiard table. I won't bother to praise the beds because after an eighteen-mile walk and a bottle of wine each, we could have slept on a pile of rubble. The evening passed pleasantly and while Madame Horel fussed over us, we in turn fussed over Peter's feet. The said feet were in a terrible state, the soles covered with large, white, bubbly blisters.

There was still no sign of Geoff. A telephone call to Britain established that he was still flat on his back but had progressed to weak tea and digestive biscuits, and the prognosis was favourable, so putting the invalids out of our minds for the evening, we settled down to enjoy ourselves with the locals, who had warmed up a bit and become quite chatty.

I found this first evening set the pattern for many other evenings on my walk across France. The locals in the bars would greet my arrival with suspicious stares or serried backs, but then quickly mellowed, progressing rapidly from indifference to hospitality. Given a little French, the lone walker in France need never be lonely for long, and even though the Normans are reputed to be one of the more dour people in France, they are used to the English and we fit together rather well.

May was once a mining town, extracting iron-ore for the foundries of the north. The seams have long since petered out and the underground galleries are now full of oil, stored as part of France's strategic reserves. Apart from iron-ore, and shining pyrites or 'fool's gold', the area is also noted for fossils. Madame Horel was keen to show us her collection of ammonites, from which her hotel took its name. We admired her collection, John and Keith played pool with the locals, Toby's beard had advanced to the stubble stage, and after dinner and a Calvados or two, Peter was feeling no pain. We went up to bed about eleven, undisturbed by the church clock across the way, which chimed on the quarter-hour throughout the night – no problem if you can get to sleep in fourteen minutes – and the rising gale that arrived in Normandy that night, after punishing the south of England and the Channel coast. Our first day had been completed, and The Walk had actually begun.

With the dawn came the Keen Rambler. The idea that I might enjoy meeting the local representatives of the *Fédération Française pour la Randonnée Pédestre* (FFRP) had been suggested early in the planning stage, at a time when I was too busy to resist. I had long since forgotten all about this projected rendezvous until I looked out of the hotel window across the rain-lashed courtyard and saw a wiry, elderly gentleman advancing towards the hotel door in a large and business-like pair of boots. This was the Keen Rambler, and his mission was to show us parts of the province that we might otherwise, with any luck, have missed.

The Keen Rambler was keen to show us, in particular, the place where William the Conqueror crossed the Orne. As William was Duke of Normandy from 1035 until 1087, and the Orne divides his duchy, it is a fair bet that he crossed the Orne quite often, but that would not do for our self-appointed guide. He became fairly insistent that one particular crossing, which lay just west of May, was a place we must not miss. I pointed out, mildly, that all I really wanted to do was walk south, and this being so, even a step in any other direction was a step wasted, but it did no good. We climbed into our wind- and water-proofs and went off down the road in a howling gale to see where 'Bill the Basher' crossed the Orne. It wasn't worth it.

Our route that day should have taken us about twenty miles up to the border of the Suisse-Normande and, with that sort of distance to cover, the most direct route seemed advisable, but the Keen Rambler had other ideas. Under his guidance there was no bank we failed to climb, no thicket left unprobed, no swamp unwaded. If he could find a track that led uphill, against the wind and preferably in the wrong direction, so much the better. Before long, the Ferrets began to mutter. It was also made clear that the Keen Rambler strongly disapproved of the well-established Ferret tradition of entering every bar we came across in the interests of our readers. He tried to divert us from this practice with loud 'halloas' and by waving us onward, but in this, at least, he failed. There were one or two compensations that morning; the first flush of spring flowers – daffodils, cowslips, and patches of primrose dotted along the hedgerows – and when the sun did come out (and it came out for all of half an hour), it brought with it big brimstone butterflies to flutter about our knees. Even so, it was a rather weary, very muddy, and bloody-minded set of Ferrets who trailed out of the woods and walked slowly up to our lunch stop at the elegant Auberge du Pont de Brie, some fifteen miles south of Caen. The Auberge lies west of the sprawling Forêt de Grimbosq, close to Goupilières, a pleasant spot where the British seem very welcome, especially if they are from the 'Cherry Pickers', the 11th Hussars, who fought a brisk little action against the Germans hereabouts in 1944, an event recorded on various memorials in and around the hotel. By now, we had emerged from the valley of the May into the valley of the Orne, and were on the edge of the Suisse-Normande, a hilly, rocky region which lies on either side of the Orne, running south from Thury-Harcourt, as far as Putanges-Pont-Ecrepin.

Quite why this area bears such an unusual name is not clear. It straddles the Armorican Massif, a region of shale and sandstone which underpins much of western Normandy, but is woefully short of high mountains, lakes and rushing rivers. The Suisse-Normande is much more like the Peak District of Derbyshire, a green, hilly, steep-sided country, traversed by the Orne, well supplied with pretty villages, perfect for the walker and even, here and there, the climber. From now on the GR36 would follow the Orne and, rather more usefully, since the river was in flood, the line of the Caen-Domfront railway. This, if the rusting track was any indication, had recently fallen out of use. Like canal tow-paths, railways are useful arteries for walkers because the track bed is flat, with tunnels cut through any steep ridges, and there are bridges to span any gaps.

When walking the Robert Louis Stevenson Trail, we used the Mimente Valley railway above Florac to make our approach to the Cévennes. That had been out of use for many years and the track had long since gone, but the bridges were still there, though they creaked alarmingly as we marched across. Eventually we sent the heaviest walker over first, protesting loudly, to see if it was up to his weight. If he survived, we followed. The Suisse-Normande railway is still used for a steam train service in summer, and a most beautiful journey it must be, through those steep gorges, cloaked in golden gorse; but unless the track receives some attention shortly, it will not remain usable for much longer.

Lunch at the Auberge du Pont de Brie went on just the right amount of time, which is to say, rather too long. We were not back on the trail again until mid-afternoon and an hour after that welcome break, the Ferrets finally mutinied against the Keen Rambler. In that hour we had climbed a hill through the Forêt de Grimbosq, battled our way against the wind along a muddy ridge, descended through a valley, hacked our way through thickets of brambles and ended up just 300 yards from our starting point. Meanwhile, the Keen Rambler had been dripping dark thoughts in Paul Armandary's ear which Paul, as a committed Ferret, had promptly relayed back to us.

'He doesn't think we're serious walkers – we do too much laughing and far too much drinking. The whisky bottles seem to unnerve him . . . and as for *you* . . . ,' Paul continued, turning to me, 'he thinks you'll never make it. He says you look old, tired and very unfit.'

I must not be too hard on the Keen Rambler because the Ferrets are not the conventional idea of a walking group. As city people, they tend to view the countryside as something to get through as quickly as possible, so that the revels can commence. The Keen Rambler, like many weekend walkers, took the whole thing much more seriously, even gloomily, and the time was not sufficient to mellow our acquaintance. The atmosphere simmered with mutual loathing. Relations between the Ferrets and the Keen Rambler hit a new low when we reached another turning off the main track, the Keen Rambler plunging up a muddy slope, the Ferrets veering sharp right onto the railway track where, ignoring all the bellows from behind, they marched rapidly round the bend and out of earshot. We saw no more of the Keen Rambler until we reached the outskirts of

Thury-Harcourt later that afternoon, when we came off the hill and met an old friend from previous Brittany walks, Monsieur Chandelier, a *Maire-Adjoint* of the town. A *Maire-Adjoint* is a deputy mayor and Monsieur Gautier, the Mayor of Thury-Harcourt, has no less than seven. Monsieur Chandelier, who knows our priorities, led us directly to the town's brand-new community centre where, it appeared, the Ferrets would enjoy a Champagne reception and I would make a speech. I was less keen on this last part of the arrangements. Speeches are not my strong point, and another of our Ferret rules is that when we are forced to respond, Peter Chambers makes the speeches. Peter has the gift of tongues but he was absent, exploring the remoter parts of Calvados in Toby Oliver's Mercedes, so that left me fully exposed.

'Just say "Thanks for having us . . ."' said Paul. 'And keep smiling.' 'Find out which one of the girls is Miss Thury-Harcourt', suggested Toby.

'Make sure we stand close to the drink,' was John's contribution.

With forty miles completed in the first two days, the evening concluded with a banquet in our hotel, the Hôtel du Val d'Orne, which lies just below all that is left of the Harcourt château, burned by the Germans on the night before they pulled out in 1944.

The banquet served the triple purpose of welcoming the *Ferrets-amis-randonneurs-de-la-Normandie,* urging me on my way – '. . . *et bon voyage et bonne chance, cher Rob'* – and enabling the town council to have a slap-up meal on the ratepayers. I sat between the *Maire* and the Lady Mayoress, wearing a smile that became ever more glazed as the meal wore on.

'I'm glad to see you are making such a big impression on the Lady Mayoress,' whispered Peter. The Lady Mayoress spent most of the meal studying catalogues of furniture for the Mayor's parlour, and all attempts at conversation came round to the merits of stripped pine or polished oak.

Thury-Harcourt, *La porte de la Suisse-Normande*, is a pleasant little town, proud of a long connection with England, one dating back to Norman times, when the Lord of Harcourt rode at William's back up Senlac hill. A large number of the locals seemed to speak English, the Champagne flowed, and the Ferrets, as always on such occasions, became extremely animated. Meanwhile, the Keen Rambler glowered at us from the corner, coming over just once to volunteer the news that, according to the *Fédération Française pour la Randonnée Pédestre* in Paris, no one had ever walked across France from the Channel coast to the Mediterranean. His tone implied that no one was going to do it this time either.

The hotel was pleasant enough and the only real snag was presented by the electrics, or to be more exact, a bare wire that jutted from the wall by the light switch in the upstairs lavatory. Groping for the light in the dark became a real experience. When anyone departed upstairs, all ears were cocked for the rattle of the door knob, the closing of the door, the short silence . . . the scream. How we escaped electrocution I will never know. The French seem to have a very cavalier attitude towards electricity; perhaps they don't really believe in it. Bare wires project from the walls or coil around the skirting boards or lie in wait in the dark, even in the most well-appointed places, but somehow no real
harm is done.

Next morning it took several large pots of coffee to revive the Ferrets, and we were still in the bar at ten o'clock, when there came a tapping on the steamy window. Outside, grinning widely at us through the glass, stood Geoff.

The winds of yesterday had blown themselves out, leaving us with a clear, bright morning in which Thury-Harcourt sparkled. Like many of the hamlets and villages hereabouts, Thury-Harcourt was severely knocked about in the Battle of Normandy in 1944, when two million men fought each other all across the province. Fortunately, when the battle passed on, the local people restored their town in the old style, avoiding the temptation to raze the ruined buildings and start again. So although largely reconstructed, it has a pleasant, time-worn air. We took a quick look at the thirteenth-century church, and passing under the ruined château of the Dukes of Harcourt, set out on the next leg of our journey. This was to Pont-d'Ouilly, in the heart of the Suisse-Normande, about fifteen miles away, leaving the GR36 to wander off on its own towards the east, up to the chapel and viewpoint of St-Joseph, high above the river.

Looking about nervously for the Keen Rambler, we set off south along the railway line. Following the tracks for a while through ever-denser bramble thickets, we climbed down through the woods to reach the River Orne and the GR36 again by the bridge at Cantepie. Near here the GR36 is joined by another long-distance path, the GR22, which comes in from the Cotentin, but we continued along the road, past a number of attractive auberges and into the town of Clécy, just in time for lunch at the Hôtel le Site Normande. Here Peter gallantly ate his way through a plate of *tripe à la mode du Caen,* a feat the rest of us watched with horror. I will eat practically anything – but not entrails.

Clécy is a pleasant little town, occupying a small knoll above the river at the head of the Orne gorges. The centre for some of the best walking in the Suisse-Normande, it has many local strolls down to the bridge at Vey, where the old millhouse is now a popular hotel, or up to the viewpoint of the Pain de Sucre, which overlooks a broad sweep of the now rain-lashed river. Fortunately, as we emerged from the hotel after lunch and began to grope about for the out-of-town waymarks, the sky cleared and the sun came out again, warming the air rapidly until the whole countryside began to steam in the sunshine. We followed the path beside the river, scrambled up the railway embankment to the top of the viaduct, and followed the track south for a while to La Lande, where we re-joined the GR36. All went well until about five, when we arrived at the hamlet of Bourg St Marc. There Toby announced that he could not go another yard without a beer and found a small café on a path beside the road. He led us inside – not to re-emerge for several hours.

Toby has a knack of finding little cafés like the one at Bourg, but the Bar des Amis was not a bar in the normal sense of the word. To begin with, there was no bar. There was a central table, a sofa, a bench or two, several chairs, a sideboard littered with bottles, a cooker and a fridge. This is the sort of place where the Ferrets feel at home, and we were warmly welcomed by Paul Angel, his neighbour Suzanne, and Max the dog. Suzanne's pretty nieces, Natalie, Stéphanie and Mérielle, came in for a look at *les Anglais,* while Paul, who is the local historian, and I, had a long discussion about the pilgrimage to Compostela, because the church at Bourg St Marc, which Paul said is properly St Mards, has a statue of St Roch dressed in pilgrim garments, bearing the *coquille de St Jacques,* the symbol of the Santiago pilgrimage.

When we emerged, after warmly embracing Natalie, Stéphanie and Mérielle, it was well after dark. So, with dinner at risk, Toby and I decided to run the last mile or two into Pont-d'Ouilly, where Peter and Geoff must by now be wondering what had happened to the walking half of the party. This run was so effective that I decided on arrival to skip dinner, and crawled upstairs to bed. There I slept for twelve solid hours, which is as good a way to end a long day's walk as any other I can think of.

Our journey next day, my final day with the Ferrets, took us high above the River Rouvrou, along the Orne gorges, and past the viewpoint of the Roche d'Oëtre, which is the greatest scenic attraction of the Suisse-Normande – though not necessarily during a wild spring day at the end of March.

'This must be the day for a picnic,' Paul had declared suddenly over breakfast.

'Why?'

'It's snowing!'

So it was. This was one of those mad March days when winter and spring are still fighting it out and winter has all the experience. During our walk we had patches of sunshine, interspersed with hail, snow and buckets of rain, but we climbed out of Pont-d'Ouilly, past the meandering Rouvrou, and set off along the crest, using footpaths that more often than not were little torrents. There is a technique for walking in such conditions; if the stream is running fast, you walk in the middle where the flow will have washed the mud away and the ground offers a firm footing. Where the path is flat and marshy and the stream slows, you skip or leap from tussock to tussock as best you can, and when all else fails, you simply plough through the swamp. Whatever happens you get wet feet.

By now we had covered some sixty miles from the coast and had rarely been dry during the day. As yet there was no real sign of spring, apart from the occasional clump of primroses, but as we reached the Roche d'Oëtre and settled down on the viewpoint above the river to polish off our last half-bottle of Scotch, the sun came briefly out and transformed the landscape. Two buzzards appeared, swooping slowly over the bare branches of the trees far below, and a small flotilla of canoeists swept past downstream, paddling hard to keep their kayaks off the rocks. The Roche d'Oëtre is a natural balcony above the Rouvrou, overlooking the forested sides of the gorge, and a popular tourist attraction complete with restaurant and souvenir shop, both of which were closed. We climbed down the rocks below the crest to get out of the wind, getting some warmth from the sun, and the day was suddenly almost blissful. The skies had cleared at last. They remained that way for several hours as we followed the GR36 to La Forêt-Auvray, through green and gentle countryside. The only snag here, and indeed for most of the walk, were the dogs. Farms or hamlets, apparently quite empty of people, were still well supplied with dogs. The hounds barked, yelped or howled at the sight of us, and kept the din going long after we had passed. I am not sure if the French actually like dogs but they certainly have a great many of them, three or four per farm at least, some loose, some tethered, some seemingly insane, all noisy. There were large dogs and small ones, pedigrees and mongrels, hounds and poodles, and on this particular morning, one curious creature, completely covered in wool, that barked so hard it finally fell over. We studied this last one closely from behind the safety of a fence. 'That's very curious,' said John at last. 'A barking sheep!'

One essential item of equipment for any walker in France is a stout walking stick. I had been presented with a very fine specimen of holly-wood with a polished goat-horn handle, and very useful it proved in fending off or discouraging even the most aggressive curs. But nothing much could be done about the noise, and incessant barking is one of the snags that a walker through France must simply accept.

Somewhere down this part of the GR36 we met a group of French ramblers, trudging slowly uphill in very state-of-the-art outdoor kit, heading for the Roche d'Oëtre. As for us, we veered off into Ménil-Hermei and La Forêt-Auvray for our picnic lunch which, since it was snowing hard again, we took in the town's seventeenth-century market hall, recently renovated for the *jeunesse* and for the use of walkers. The Ferrets stood hopefully sniffing the air outside the kitchen of yet another Bar des Amis – where a huge family lunch was in progress on this Sunday morning – but our picnic in the market hall was still a great success. Given that we had good food, good company, and an endless supply of wine, this was not too surprising. It was well into the afternoon before we got under way again, walking through the woods above the windy gorges of St Aubert where, what with one thing and another, we got completely lost. This was partly due to my 'sudden' discovery that ten pages of the *topo-guide* were missing, partly due to the fact that the map scale was too small, and partly due to the lunch. The cumulative effect was to infuriate Geoff. 'Look Rob, if you're ever going to get to the Med, you've got to stop all this stumbling about, lost in the woods, and really get to grips with the map reading.'

The Ferrets were shocked. Stumbling about, getting lost in the woods and mountains is what the Brittany Walk is all about – if you want reliability take a package tour. However, Geoff in a rage is a fearful thing, so we got out the compass, set it due south, and began to plough directly across country, through woods and fields, crawling under fences, impaling ourselves on barbed wire, tantalised from time to time by GR36 waymarks which appeared frequently for a few hundred metres, then simply petered out again. That tends to be the way with GR waymarks, and their presence or absence reflects either the proximity of the nearest road, the enthusiasm or otherwise of the local waymarkers, or a sudden shortage of red and white paint. Whatever the reason, this hit and miss waymarking can be most confusing and vastly irritating at the end of a tiring day. Quite often, following a clear, obvious track, one without the slightest possibility of error, those red and white paint slashes would appear on every post and stone. On the other hand, reach a five-lane track divergence in the middle of the darkest wood, and there won't be a waymark in sight. The only real solution to this problem is constant use of the map, the *topo-guide* and, if need be, the compass. That, together with occasional help from the waymarks, will get you where you want to go with no more than a small amount of fuss. Over the next few weeks I learned the basic rule of map reading again and again – always know where you are. On the other hand I forgot this Golden Rule just as often, emerging from some pleasant daydream to find myself yet again totally lost. I must have walked an extra hundred miles because of this hit-or-miss waymarking.

Waymarking is an art, and like all arts, is one open to error. Simple error is compounded by the fact that, while the trails are waymarked by people who know the area, the marks are followed in the main by strangers, who often need a little more help than the local people feel it necessary to provide. In actual fact, I got seriously lost only once during this walk across France, and that was when I entrusted my route to a group of French *randonneurs* south of Châteauroux. They took me miles out of my way, then left me by the roadside in gathering dusk, leaping into their cars to drive home. After that I did get a grip on the map reading and flatly refused to be diverted from my path by any local suggestions. My road lay south, always south, only south, to the far blue Mediterranean Sea, and no diversions, however tempting, were allowed. Well, hardly any.

Dusk was falling, assisted by a thin rain, as we finally emerged from the woods and came out onto the escarpment overlooking Putanges, to weave our way through a few more fields and come down to the Hôtel du Cerf Verd by the river. It was a rather less welcoming *logis* than those we had encountered up to now, but perhaps our wet clothes, muddy boots and dishevelled appearance had something to do with it. My own appearance was particularly unpleasant, because in addition to looking more than usually bedraggled after eighty muddy miles across the Suisse-Normande, one eye was completely bloodshot, and the other purpling up rapidly after a blow in the face from a branch. With Peter's blisters, Geoff's toes and my wild eyes, fifty per cent of us were wounded. 'Look on the bright side,' said Peter, as I keened over my wounds in the mirror. 'At least you won't be hard to identify. There can't be many people walking across France with one red eye and one black one. But since it's our last evening together, let's send you on your way with some Champagne.'

They do serve very good food at the Cerf Verd, and it is surprising what a hot bath, a meal and a bottle or three of wine can do to revive flagging spirits, even when you know that you have it all to do again on the morrow. All things considered, this first leg of our journey, across the Caen plain and the Suisse-Normande, had gone more or less according to plan. We had walked about eighty miles and made a small but useful dent in the overall distance. Even if I still felt quite exhausted at the end of each day, I must be getting fitter – mustn't I? The weather was not too promising but that lay outside our control, and so far we had concentrated, quite successfully, on getting to the next night-stop and having a good time. Now the Ferrets were heading home, while Geoff and I had to increase the pace a little and arrow due south for the Loire. The time had come to put away the corkscrew and get down to some serious walking.

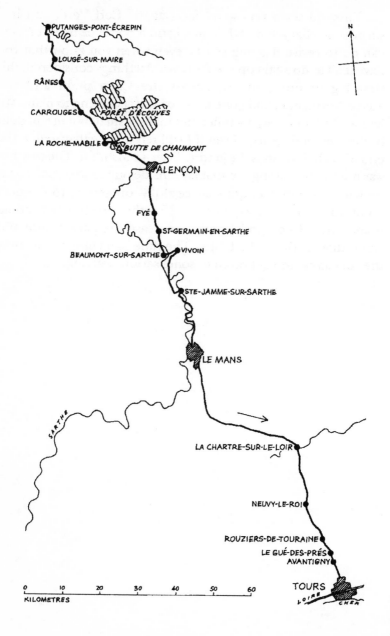

PUTANGES-PONT-ÉCREPIN
LOUGÉ-SUR-MAIRE
RÂNES
CARROUGES
FORÊT D'ÉCOUVES
LA ROCHE-MABILE
BUTTE DE CHAUMONT
ALENÇON
FYÉ
ST-GERMAIN-EN-SARTHE
BEAUMONT-SUR-SARTHE
VIVOIN
STE-JAMME-SUR-SARTHE
LE MANS
SARTHE
LA CHARTRE-SUR-LE-LOIR
NEUVY-LE-ROI
ROUZIERS-DE-TOURAINE
LE GUÉ-DES-PRÉS
AVANTIGNY
TOURS
LOIRE
CHER

N

0   10   20   30   40   50   60
KILOMETRES

CHAPTER THREE

SOUTH TO THE LOIRE

'The great and recurring question about abroad is,
is it worth the trouble of getting there?'
Rose Macaulay

As Geoff and I walked out of Putanges-Pont-Ecrepin next morning, the rain was falling steadily. For the first hour we kept to the rutted verge of the main road and were frequently wreathed in spray as great *camions* shot past, each one dragging a lurching trailer. We were a mile or so out of town before the Ferrets swept by, taking Geoff's car down to our night-stop at Carrouges.

'When we passed you that morning, God, it looked miserable,' Peter told me later. 'Grey skies, steady rain, dripping trees, a chill wind, and there you were, trudging along – at least Geoff had an umbrella.' Geoff owed his umbrella, as well as his feet and most of his clothing, to the Maidenhead Rugby Club, of which he is a devoted member, and it attracted a considerable amount of attention, and looked rather odd. The French are not used to umbrellas and I am not at all sure that umbrellas, however useful, are the proper equipment for a serious walker, besides being quite impractical in the woods. I must admit, however, that I was more than happy to edge under it when the rainstorms swept in. A little south of Putanges-Pont-Ecrepin we turned off the road onto the GR36 once again, while the rain settled down to a steady, persistent, all-day drizzle that soon had us soaked to the skin.

In spite of the weather, passing Putanges-Pont-Ecrepin brought us a little victory, for in doing so we passed from the Norman *département* of Calvados, a land of farms and apple orchards, into the forested *département* of the Orne. Our task now was to head south out of Normandy altogether, into the flatlands of the Sarthe, and to reach the Loire on time in another six days. To this task we presently applied ourselves, and increased the pace.

Rain apart, it was a pleasant morning to be walking through the woods. The cowslips were a little more in evidence, there was spring-song from the birds: the rooks were cawing as they flew to and fro, building their nests in the swaying tops of the taller trees, and the occasional machine-gun rattle of a woodpecker came from somewhere deeper in the woods. The sight of a tree-creeper scuttling round a trunk, searching for insects in the bark, helped to divert our thoughts from the cold water trickling down our spines. Forest tracks make for pleasant, soft walking, and we made good time into the little village of Lougé-sur-Maire, arriving there just before noon, in need of a drink and a snack.

Lougé-sur-Maire was like a graveyard. It was Monday and most French villages are quiet on Mondays, which seems to have replaced Sunday as the day of rest. On a Sunday in France, everything is open except for the bank, and even street markets are not uncommon, but on Mondays everything, including the bank, tends to be shut. We walked down streets lined with shuttered houses into the central square by the church without meeting a soul, and were rattling the locked door of a bar when the church bell burst into clamour above our heads, filling the empty streets with a sudden, shattering noise. Even the air shook.

'That's the Angelus,' bellowed Geoff, his hands over his ears.

'The what?' I shouted back.

'It's twelve o'clock . . . .' He pointed to the tower. 'The Angelus bell – any good Catholic knows that.'

I didn't know that Geoff was a Catholic – and I've known him for more than twenty years – but this rainswept, din-filled street was no place to develop the subject. Besides, I felt like lunch. Lunch is not easy to find on Monday in a French village. The sleepy quietness of these rural communities was one of the smaller problems I encountered almost daily on the walk when, from time to time, I needed pointing in the right direction: there was never anyone to ask. Quite often I would walk all day, passing through small hamlets or quite large villages, and see not a soul and so it was here in Lougé. We tried the doors of another café near the *Mairie,* and found them firmly locked, then headed across the rainswept square towards a restaurant, Le Pluton, which turned out to be open, hospitable and more than willing to whip up an omelette and a *pichet* of *vin rouge.* The bar was full of farmers, stout, red-faced fellows in working *bleu* and muddy boots, who stared at us intently for several minutes and then became very helpful when we asked directions – or rather they would have been helpful if I could have understood their accent, and they could have read my map. By and large, it is no good showing country people a map. They don't need maps and they can't usually follow them, but after a little conversation we could more or less figure out our way back to the southern footpath.

We dawdled an hour away at the Pluton over our omelette, some fruit, a little cheese and the wine before we felt ready to press on again. The rain was now no more than a thin drizzle, the sun was putting in a fitful appearance, and we spent a fairly peaceful afternoon, interrupted only once near Rines, when a large boxer dog rushed out to bite me and had to be beaten off with my walking stick. We arrived in Carrouges at five, having walked for seven hours and covered a useful nineteen miles. Geoff, rightly, felt very pleased with this performance, but I just felt tired. After five days on the trail, Geoff's attrition factor was starting to take effect. It took me fifteen minutes to get my boots off, and my legs stiffened up alarmingly whenever I sat down.

Carrouges is a pleasant little town, especially when the evening sun is shining, and our night stop, the Hôtel du Nord, a one-star *logis,* was comfortable enough, though rather too full of dogs. We draped every available radiator with wet clothing, and went down to dinner where, it says here in my notebook, we had fried elvers (small eels), the speciality of the house, before stepping out for a stroll – or in my case a hobble – round the empty streets.

Carrouges is the central town for the sprawling Parc Normandie-Maine, a vast, forested region which straddles the frontier between the Norman duchy and the old county of Mayenne. The town's chief attraction is the castle of Le Veneur de Tillières. The de Tillières family lived hereabouts from the twelfth century until 1936, when their castle was handed over to the state. The present castle, which stands on the site of a medieval *château-fort,* dates from the time of Henri IV, the late sixteenth century, but although a Renaissance château, it was built for defence and is moated. I like castles, and the castle of Carrouges is quite splendid, especially when bathed in the evening sunlight. We took this in, checked on the dark, big-bellied rain clouds still sweeping in from the west, and went to bed.

Next morning I couldn't walk. I managed to get out of bed and could stand well enough, but when it came to moving one foot in front of the other and making for the bathroom, my legs refused to function. I reeled about the room, clutching the walls and furniture, while Geoff watched from his bed, doubled up with laughter.

'You should see yourself,' he chortled. 'You poor old bastard. How are you going to reach the Med when you can't even reach the bathroom?'

This performance was repeated on most mornings during the walk. I had hoped and imagined that once I got fit I would be as nimble as a spring lamb, but it didn't work out like that. My legs were always stiff and painful until the muscles slackened and began to warm up, but in the end there was something almost pleasant about the morning warm-up. I would stagger into the bathroom like a man of ninety and emerge, post-shower, like one of . . . well . . . fifty, and after breakfast I was usually more than ready for the road.

There is another small snag posed by a hike across France: walking can become an end in itself, and that is just not good enough. I still wanted to see the sights, particularly the castles. France runs to two kinds of castle: the large, ornate variety which he along the Loire are *châteaux,* and the word is often used to describe the building which the British might call a manor or even a country house. The proper medieval castle, with crenellated walls and towers, is a *château-fort.* Given the choice, I prefer *the château-fort* variety every time.

The gatehouse of the castle at Carrouges, which was built to protect the town on the hill above from any force marching up from the valley of the River Maine further south – is the most striking feature of the place, so we drove down there and took a few photographs before returning to Carrouges itself.

While Geoff went to pack, I set off for our next stop, Alençon. Following our original plan, Geoff would have come over with the rest of us and therefore been without his car. As it was, having the car was a good thing, because it could transport our luggage and, when he had done enough walking for the day, Geoff could act as support team for the lone, wet walker. I still intended to avoid humping that heavy rucksack for as long as possible, and having the car put off the evil moment for another six days.

By now we were well off the GR36, which had rambled away to the east into the Forêt d'Ecouves, so I decided to follow a minor 'D' road south for the first seven miles on a pleasant, rolling route through the Parc Normandie-Maine. I had been on the road for about an hour when I saw before me, but still far away, a high, distinctive hill. Walkers in France soon learn that if there is a distinctive hill feature on the path, then the path itself will surely go right over the top. Checking the map, I saw that this must be the Butte de Chaumont on the GR36, a high, humped hill, running up to just over the 1,000-foot mark. When I reached the little village of La Roche-Mabile, below the Butte, the GR36 came wandering up from the east like an old friend, and a quick check of waymarks showed them leading towards the Butte. So far, so good. At this moment, Geoff drew up alongside in his car and suggested that we meet on the top for a picnic. He set off to buy the wherewithal and then drive round to the foot of the hill, while I struck out directly up the footpath. I didn't see him again until the middle of the afternoon.

From La Roche-Mabile the GR36 path fell away downhill, crossed a stream, then rose fairly gently towards the edge of the Butte de Chaumont, where stood a small chapel. I skirted this and, with one finger on the map to note my position, ploughed on carefully through the wood towards the Butte. France has many such forests and some are of considerable size, all of them seamed with wide, dividing 'rides'. These are swathes cut through the forest, serving partly as firebreaks and partly to let the loggers in to extract timber. Although these rides make for easy walking, new ones are being cut all the time and only the main ones appear on the maps. It is therefore all too easy to get lost. I got to our rendezvous at the foot of the hill and waited there for fifteen minutes. Then, since Geoff had still not arrived, I decided to climb the Butte de Chaumont but, failing to find the easy way up, I shinned up the steep, rocky face of the Butte. Sprawled tight against the rock, scrabbling for toe-holds, I finally crawled over the top – onto the footpath, of course. The Butte de Chaumont stands out high above the surrounding country, and on a fine day must offer great views south to Alençon and out of Normandy. This is a guess, because hail and snow came beating in as I circled my way up to the top, the hailstones rattling sharply on my windproofs, and stinging my face.

Having got up there, with nothing in sight but sodden fields and drifts of rain, there was nothing to do but come down again. Much shouting and whistling failed to produce Geoff, who was shouting and whistling for me on the other side of the Butte. Cursing him soundly, I set off again down one of the rides, pleasant walking on soft ground, through the empty forest. Two deer suddenly appeared, leaping startlingly into view about 50 yards ahead, bounding silendy across the path into the undergrowth. The rain was now settling in in earnest, so I struggled deeper into my windproofs, which kept the rain out for all of five minutes, and set out to walk off the distance as fast as possible into the town of Alençon. Half an hour after I left the forest, Geoff came sweeping up again, and lured me onward with a bottle of *rouge*, all the way to the city.

Alençon lies on the main railway line running south from Caen to Tours, and from there the railway would parallel my path all the way to the Loire. This would enable us to leave Geoff's car during the day, from now on, provided we stopped somewhere down the line each evening and he could return to collect it. We worked this out over a coffee in the buffet, and since the rain had stopped, as it tended to do once the walking was over, we set off to explore the town.

Alençon is one of my favourite Norman towns. A little city on the Sarthe, with a fine, rather ornate Gothic cathedral, it also boasts, near the park, the towers of the *château-fort* built by Jean, Duc d'Alençon, in the fifteenth century. The dukes of Alençon lived in considerable state here until the time of the Revolution, so that, as is the way with old towns, Aleçon has retained a slightly regal air, and some very fine buildings. These vary from the *Halle aux Blés*, a fine rotunda built as a market hall in 1808 and now used as a sports and dance centre, to the attractive fifteenth-century *Maison d'Ozé,* which contains the local museum. Less attractive was the sight of a pink-haired Algerian punk, who was happily pissing against the wall when we came out, his studded leather jacket emblazoned with the hopeful slogan, in English, 'Death to Humanity'. The French seem to go in for alfresco urination; when we looked out of our hotel window next morning, our first sight was of one of the guests standing below us in the catpark, happily peeing into a rose bed, although a perfectly good indoor lavatory was only a few steps away.

Alençon itself is well worth exploring, being both a market town (hence the *Halle aux Blés)* and a centre for lace-making – *le point d'Alençon.* Lace was first produced at Alençon at the end of the seventeenth century and much encouraged by Colbert, finance minister to Louis XIV. The lacemakers soon developed their own unique stitch, a pattern of flowers on a rectangular base, which is employed by the ladies of the School of Lace in Alençon to this very day. Marie-Antoinette's wedding veil was of Alençon lace, and Napoleon ordered some for Josephine and more later for his unloving Austrian Empress. The much restored castle of the Dukes is now a prison and, although Alençon was considerably knocked about in 1944, especially during the tank battles around the Falaise gap, and heavily shelled when General Leclerc's Armoured Brigade liberated the town in August, it has been carefully rebuilt, like most of these war-ravaged Norman towns. The raw patches have already mellowed to match the older stone, that soft Caen stone which was also used to build the Tower of London and the Cathedral at Canterbury.

Like Clécy, Alençon is a good centre for outdoor lovers. Just to the east lies the Perseigne Forest, and to the west the GR22 comes in along the long ridge cloaked by the Forêt de Multonne to the Mont des Avaloirs, the highest point in western France 1,368 feet – before joining the GR36 near St Denis. Geoff went up the Mont des Avaloirs to find a view and found instead the local hunt up there in force, all in red coats hung about with brass French horns. South-west of Alençon lie the Alpes-Mancelles which resemble the mighty Alps as much as the Suisse-Normande recalls Switzerland. But they still offer good walking and can be explored on a *variante* of the GR36, *Le Tour des Alpes-Mancelles*. This countryside, straddling the frontier of Normandy, is an amalgamation of the duchy and the county of Maine, a region where quite low hills give vast views, and quite large villages are tucked out of sight in the deep slashes cut by the rivers. Walking south, at the end of March, much of this fine countryside was obscured by the sweeping drifts of rain, but Geoff and I returned through here by car on our way home in May, at a time when the sun was shining. Given that touch of sunshine, the countryside was all green fields, flat plain and deep forests, set about with small, biscuit-coloured villages, and quite beautiful. . . . I must go there again.

Wednesday morning brought some brief sunshine and 1 April, All Fools Day, *le Poisson d'Avril.* I had now been walking for seven days and we had covered about 130 miles, a fairly satisfying statistic. It also brought Geoff down to breakfast, full of beans and wearing a rugby shirt, engagingly emblazoned with the title 'Groin Stompers'.

'Very tasteful,' I observed, sourly. 'Where did that come from?' 'It's our Boxing Day Rugby Team shirt. What's the programme for today?' Our programme called for another serious walk.

To reach the Loire at Tours by Saturday we would have to press on and cover the remaining distance, of just under 100 miles, at a fairly fast gallop. This meant daily stages of at least twenty miles, and more if I could do it – through Beaumont-sur-Sarthe, Le Mans, La Chartre-sur-le-Loir and, all being well, into Tours. If we could reach Tours by Saturday evening, I could award myself a day off. If I could not, we had a problem, for Geoff had to go back on the Sunday, which would add my rucksack to my problems. Much of this walking would be on forest tracks or minor roads, for my axis, the GR36, had gone for yet another wander to the west, but I must head south, and put my foot down. As we started, it began to rain again.

I have to say that by now I was getting somewhat fed up with the weather. If you go walking, you have to accept whatever the weather throws at you, but this northern part of France needs fine weather to compensate for terrain that is, by and large, somewhat lacking in drama. Wild weather in wild country can be exciting; rain on the plain is simply dreary. Geoff voiced this thought as we walked out of Alençon towards Fyé, under a leaden sky and through field after field of dripping cabbages.

'How are you going to describe this lot?' he asked, gesturing around at the mist-wreathed countryside. 'Maybe you should give up this part of the walk and take the train to the sun – or at least to the next piece of decent scenery.'

'No – I've got to walk all the way. That's the project, so that's what I've got to do. What you suggest isn't a bad idea, but if I start copping out just because we get a little wet, what happens when it really gets nasty?'

I really believe this. Discomfort is only relative, and it is quite surprising what you can get used to. No one has less objection to comfort and good living than I have, but you enjoy the good things far more if you experience a little misery on the way towards them. Splashing along in the rain rates a lot better than putting on wet socks in a snowhole or sitting in a trench while it fills with water from the bottom and snow from the top, but I've met most of my best friends in such unlikely situations. Geoff wasn't actually objecting to the weather, which he can endure as well as me, but to the fact that nothing much was happening.

At that moment a tractor eased past, the driver jerking his head invitingly at the small cart he was towing behind. I waved my thanks but also waved him on.

'Now, I would have said that was legitimate,' said Geoff, 'and it might even have given you a story. . . .'

'Get thee behind me, Satan,' I said, 'and let's take a look at this church.'

The church at St-Germain-en-Sarthe is well worth a visit. It has a fine Romanesque door, a medieval tower and a barrel-vault to the nave. I like the Romanesque architecture, which is roughly contemporaneous with the Norman architecture of England. The Romanesque is not all that common in northern France where, since Romanesque churches tended to fall down, they were often replaced with the Gothic style, pioneered by Archbishop Suger in the Ile de France. Early medieval builders had great difficulty with church roofs, for to support any sort of span, the church walls had to be very thick. Even so, both the weight of the roof and the low profile needed to span the nave tended to push the walls out. When Archbishop Suger was constructing his Church of St Denis outside Paris, he ordered his masons to let in the light and raise the roof. In doing so they made the interesting discovery that if the roof vault was pointed, then the weight of the roof went downwards, through the walls to the foundations, and so the Gothic style developed. Walls could be higher, thinner, and pierced by windows, although the extent to which verticality could be carried out was discovered only by trial and error; towers often fell down and the walls still had to be supported by flying buttresses. The later Gothic churches, once these problems had been solved, are light, airy masterpieces, but I still like the good solid feel of the Romanesque. There would be more examples of this style later, as we got further south into the Languedoc.

We came out onto the main N138 road somewhere above Beaumont, and lunched at the Relais Napoléon at La Route, leaving muddy footprints and trails of water behind us as we headed across the bar into the restaurant. We had left Normandy behind, just outside Alençon, and south of La Route the country flattens out and the River Sarthe begins a long series of meanders, which brought it again and again across our path, spilling over the banks to flood the fields, frequently driving us off the comfortable, if muddy, footpaths back onto the hard road. Road walking is best avoided by the long-distance walker, since tarmac is eventually painful to the feet, but like the countryside itself, the minor roads of France are usually empty, with hardly a car an hour to force us into the hedgerow. Beaumont came into sight in mid-afternoon, but as is the way with footpaths, it took another couple of hours before we actually reached it, crossing the bridge into the town to discover, inevitably, that we still had another mile to do to reach our hotel, which lay at Vivoin by the railway station. We hurried to the station, as Geoff still had to catch the train back to Alençon and collect the car, and while he departed for the north, I slopped across the road and entered the hotel.

The Hôtel du Chemin de Fer at Beaumont is delightful, and Monsieur Hary, who was awaiting my arrival in the bar, was hospitality itself, assisting me out of my sopping anorak and into a a glass of Calvados without further delay. The snag was that after ten minutes sitting at the bar, my legs seized up again, and climbing the stairs to our room on the second floor was a long, slow and painful business, as Geoff discovered for himself when he tried it an hour or so later, burdened with two heavy rucksacks.

'I drove back down our route,' he declared, hurling the rucksacks into a corner, 'and it's over twenty miles. I've walked twenty miles! I haven't walked that far – well, ever! What's the matter with you?'

'I think my legs are going to drop off.'

'Then I think we'd better get you into a hot bath.'

When we limped down to dinner, the only other guests were a large party of English people *en route* for the Dordogne, and in the best traditions of the English abroad, we studiously ignored each other throughout the evening, although they were clearly dying to know what we were up to and why Monsieur Hary was being so attentive. Had they been French, they would simply have asked, but that isn't the English way.

Riding my bicycle across Spain some years ago, I arrived at the splendid *parador* in Sigüenza, hot, dirty and sweaty after a long day in the saddle, and not a pretty sight at all, standing in that elegant foyer. Fortunately, the head porter turned out to be a keen cyclist and was delighted to greet me and inspect my beautiful black, hand-made Evans machine, claiming (wisely) that such a fine cycle was best kept in my bedroom, lest curious fingers should fiddle with it. He summoned his troops to assist me, and a stage procession then crossed the crowded dining room. In front was a small *mozo* in a green suit and pillbox hat, wheeling my cycle. Behind him came two even smaller *mozo*, each carrying a pannier, and behind them the head porter, resplendent in his uniform, and myself, covered in dust. As we progressed down the room, discussing cogs and sprockets, the English guests, embarrassed, buried their faces in their plates or murmured, 'Don't look now, darling, but...' to each other across the table. The French, still chewing, turned to stare. The Spaniards stood on their chairs to get a better view. Five minutes later I was lying on my bed, groaning, when there came a tap on the door and the smallest *mozo* entered with a bottle of chilled wine, compliments of the front desk, and a handful of dusters. While I drank the wine, he polished my bicycle. That's what I call service.

Next morning, with both of us feeling rather the worse for wear, Geoff decided to leave the car at the Hôtel du Chemin de Fer and walk with me towards Le Mans and, with Monsieur Hary waving from the doorway, we creaked off down the road just after nine. It was already raining; usually it began to rain only by mid-morning and would then continue throughout the afternoon, but by twelve o'clock on this day we were already soaked through and Geoff was decidedly fed up.

'This is mad,' he said, suddenly. 'It's pissing down. You can't see a thing. We've walked bloody miles through fields of cabbages and I want a drink and a meal. Let's hitch a lift to the next village and get our feet in the trough. What do you say?'

'Never! You know what they say: "When the going gets tough the tough get going"!'

'Is that right?' I could hear his teeth grinding in the rain.

'That's right. Remember that "It isn't the size of the dog in the fight, it's the size of the fight in the dog". Hah!'

Geoff stopped, took me by the arm, and turned to face me. 'One more piece of homely philosophy like that,' he said slowly, the rain dripping off his beard, 'and I shall knee you sharply in the groin.'

We splashed on, under dreary skies, into the village of Ste-Jamme-sur-Sarthe where, after casting about in several bars, we came to rest in Cathy and Fredo's Café des Routiers in the Place de l'Eglise. Here our day brightened up no end and after ten minutes we could happily have spent the rest of the afternoon there. Lunch was in progress as we entered, with all the clientèle seated together at long tables, but they shifted up and passed the wine, the food arrived and the conversation became general, as our walking exploits produced a gratifying amount of attention and free Calvados from Fredo. Half the clientèle of the Café des Routiers seemed to have the run of the bar, going behind the counter to help themselves to a beer under a large notice saying, *'Il est interdi de faire le con'*, and nobody seemed to worry much about the money. It was actually quite hard to pay. Geoff, whose French is – to say the least – minimal, was soon deep in conversation with a very large lady in pinafore and gumboots who, with her husband, was here to assist their son, an apprentice fishmonger, at his mobile fish stall down the street. All three were putting away the *pinard* at an impressive rate.

'What's she saying?' asked Geoff, jerking my sleeve.

'She says fish is very *bon pour la force.* You know – it gets you going. I think she fancies you.'

'Tell her we'll buy a halibut. How's my French?'

'Coming on. You and Madame have reached the point of mutual incomprehension. She can't understand your questions and you can't understand her replies. Keep it up.'

By the end of an hour or so we were one very happy family. By the end of two hours, Geoff and the fish-lady were practically engaged. When we reeled out in the middle of the afternoon for a group photo with the crowd, they sent us on our way with a cheer and we felt on top of the world.

It's amazing,' said Geoff suddenly, half au hour later. 'This morning I felt really fed up and shattered – now I feel wonderful.' That's the way it goes on a long walk. As we used to say in the Commandos, much of the effort is in the heart and the mind, and the afternoon passed easily enough. Geoff peeled off about four o'clock to catch the train back to Beaumont, while I ploughed on towards Le Mans, having arranged to meet him on the first bridge inside the city. This appeared to be no great distance away, for we could by now see the taller buildings and the cathedral spire on the far horizon, but once again actually getting there was a different matter. We were now back on the footpath, but the GR36 takes a wide hook around Le Mans, so I took a minor road heading directly into the city. Soon, though, I found my way blocked by the Paris-Brest motorway, which forced me to walk miles to the west before I could find a way across. Then I got tangled up in a maze of roads through the commercial suburbs, and lost more time there. Getting to the rendezvous took far too long and I had barely arrived at the bridge, to lie groaning on the grass beside the road, when Geoff puffed up alongside. That night, I was so tired I could barely make it down to dinner, and Geoff, who had been quietly nursing me along like a Dutch uncle, was clearly concerned.

'Don't you think you ought to stop for a few days and rest?'
'I'll yomp on. You know what Robert Kennedy said: "First you
bite off more than you can chew – and then you chew it".'

'Well, you've bitten off more than you can chew all right.
Look at you – you're getting too old for this.'

'Maybe, but I shall be younger in the morning.'

'You won't have to wait that long.' It was at this point that
Geoff called upon the techniques developed by galloping out on
to rugby pitches with bucket and wet towel to revive some hulking
youth, and honed to a fine edge while looking after me on this
walk. He was going to get me to the Med if it killed him, and
ferreting in his Rugby Coach First Aid Kit – which would have
stocked half the pharmacies in the Third World – Geoff produced
a bent tube of embrocation. When he began to massage it into
my calves, the effect was like dipping them in lava – and how that
ointment stank! Days later, people in restaurants looked around
when I entered and then kicked their dog. But it got me off my
back that evening and down the stairs to dinner.

You learn a lot about your friends on a long-distance walk, and
as Geoff dropped me off on the outskirts of Le Mans next
morning, I learned his secret vice; Geoff likes to drive at high
speed around motor-racing tracks, in his sports saloon. This is
not an activity I care for.

'While you're on the plod,' he said, 'I shall have a whack at
the 24-Hour Race circuit. I hear you can get up to a hundred or
more down the Mulsanne Straight, even in my car. Do you want
to come? You can't really want to miss a blitz round the 24-Hour
Race track – you owe it to your readers.'

The Le Mans 24-Hour Endurance Race started in 1923 and
is still one of the great events of the motor-racing calendar, taking
place not on a specially built racing circuit, but on roads, which
are open to the public at all other times of the year. The
nine-mile circuit lies just south of the town and is actually crossed

by the GR36, but this was one invitation I found easy to decline, for even on a normal day, Geoff's driving is of the white knuckle variety. I watched him roar off into the rain and turned to walk south to La Chartre.

Le Mans is an old town, dating back to Roman times, and the birthplace of one of England's greatest kings, Henry II, the first Plantagenet monarch. Le Mans was Henry's favourite city, and he retreated here when his sons rebelled against him; his heir, Richard Coeur de Lion, actually drove his father from the town. Le Mans has long since sprawled out from the medieval *cité* on the hill, but the old parts are still well preserved, with a magnificent cathedral dedicated to St Julien. This, apart from a vast amount of stained glass, contains the tomb of Queen Berengaria, Richard Lionheart's much neglected spouse. She was granted the county of Maine as a dower by the King of France after the English had been driven out of France for the first time, following the battle at Bovines in 1214. In the cathedral precincts stands a small house which once belonged to the poet and writer Paul Scarron. *His* wife, Françoise, became Louis XIV's most enduring mistress and, finally, his morganatic wife, Madame de Maintenon. I could have lingered longer in Le Mans, but as always, time was pressing.

There were still fifty miles to go before Tours and, as I had only two days left to get there, I set off at a brisk clip for La Chartre-sur-le-Loir, moving a little easier, minute by minute, as my legs warmed up. just after eleven I was in St-Mars-d'Outille with eleven miles already done of the twenty-five or so I had to do that day. The church of St Mars bears a plaque to Lieutenant Clement Maudet of the French Foreign Legion, who died in the Legion's great fight at Camerone in Mexico, during Napoleon III's abortive attempt to put Maximillian on the throne there. This seemed a strange memorial to find here in the green heart of France, but even stranger, there was no sign of Geoff. This was a worry – if he had crashed on the Mulsanne Straight, the walk was over. I hung about by the church for half an hour or so, then decided that although Geoff was still absent, I might as well have lunch. I was striding cheerfully out of town in the early afternoon when he finally came swishing past.

'Where have you been?' I asked. 'I was beginning to think you'd crashed.'

'No – I got up to about a hundred and fifteen on the Mulsanne Straight but there was really too much traffic – the Nürburg Ring is much better. But I met the fish-lady again in Le Mans market – what a place! You can find everything there, from a man selling housing plots to some down-trodden peasant, standing in a puddle behind half a dozen cheeses. Write that down, why don't you?' 'Stop changing the subject. How was your girl-friend?' 'Still crazy about me.'

A little way south of St-Mars I got two more intimations that I was actually getting somewhere on this walk; I passed my first vineyard and I saw my first swallow. just one bird, swaying and bedraggled on a drip-fringed telephone wire, but it cheered me up considerably. That evening, I also passed out of the Sarthe, crossing the river into the *département* of the Loir. This is the small, masculine Loir, a distant cousin of the mighty Madame Loire, but still an extremely welcome landmark when, after a very long day indeed, I arrived on the north bank. I took a deep breath and crossed the bridge to climb the last hill into La Chartre-sur-le-Loir.

La Chartre-sur-le-Loir is a pleasant enough town but the Hôtel de France is a real gem. Monsieur Pasteau, who runs this delightful inn, is the third generation of his family to have owned it. He hopes his line will continue, for his son is also in the business as a chef, though currently resident in Montreal, Canada – a long way from this quiet little town in the valley of the Loir.

'Perhaps he will return. This is his home – but who knows? Children have their own lives to lead, but I hope. . . .'

Once a year the Hôtel de France becomes home to the racing drivers who compete in the 24-Hour Race at Le Mans. The walls of the hotel bar and restaurant are covered with their photographs – Stirling Moss, Jack Brabham, Mike Hawthorn, Jackie Ickx, all the famous *pilotes*, and Monsieur Pasteau was full of tales of their all-night parties back in the good old, gone-by days, taking us on a tour of the walls to point out the great men. 'When they had the Le Mans start – you know – when the cars were on one side and the drivers had to run across the track and jump into the cockpit – Stirling Moss was always the first away, he ran so fast. The parties here lasted often half the night, always until one or two in the morning – with much Champagne, wonderful! Now, of course, it is more serious.'

A couple of drinks with Monsieur Pasteau revived me considerably, and when he went off to see to dinner, Geoff and I went upstairs to shower and change. We were standing about stark-naked when the bedroom door swung suddenly open, sending us leaping into towels, and there in the doorway stood Sam.

Sam was just three and in his pyjamas. We chatted to him in French for some minutes before he said who he was and, since he showed no inclination to go back to bed, we finished dressing and took him down to dinner, handing him over to his family, the Powneys, which was a fortunate meeting because, like Geoff and me, the Powneys are in the book business. This gave us plenty to talk about after Sam had been persuaded back to bed, but since I am a writer, Geoff a publisher, and the Powneys booksellers, we thought it safer to discuss the customers.

'They ask such amazing questions,' said Mrs Powney. 'I had a lady come in last week and she said she didn't mind what sort of book she bought but it must have words in it.'

Geoff had another tale. 'I remember a woman who came into my wife's shop and asked if we had anything on looking after old people. When my wife said no, the woman said, "Well, all right, what have you got on euthanasia?"'

Running down the readers kept us busy until after dinner – a marvellous meal incidentally – when the Pasteaus invited us to visit their *cave*. The Pasteau wine *cave*, a long, low, hair-brushing tunnel, is cut deep into the soft *tufa* limestone of the Loir valley. A mile outside the town, it is a damp and chill place but well stocked with the local wine, Jasnières. I had never heard of it, even though, according to the brochure, Cumousky, 'Le Prince des Gastronomes' has declared that '*Trois fois par siècle, le vin de Jasnières est le meilleur vin du monde*', but then I've never heard of Cumousky either.

We polished off a bottle of Jasnières in Monsieur Pasteau's *cave*, and a bottle of Champagne back at the Hôtel de France, but all things considered, we were fairly bright in the morning when everyone assembled for breakfast in the bar. The Powneys were willingly recruited to my support team and agreed to accompany Geoff in his car for about twelve miles to the south, and bring him back to join me on this last push to the Loire. That settled, after shaking hands with the Pasteaus, I set off for the great river, still nearly thirty miles away.

It was a pleasant day – what little I can remember of it. I forced the pace hard towards Touraine, up and over the first hill from the Loir to Beaumont, then up again, out onto the wide Touraine plateau, past more vineyards and into Neuvy-le-Roi, and on to Rouziers-de-Touraine. Touraine . . . that meant another stage achieved. I had now definitely left the north and arrived in central France, even if the towers of Tours, the city of St Martin, refused to come into sight. I pressed on, swaying down the grassy verges, with storm clouds sweeping in regularly from the west to send hailstones rattling against my windproofs. As the day wore on, small villages came past one by one, hauling down the distance a kilometre at a time. Feet aching, I marched past Le Gué-des-Prés where Geoff left me, and Avantigny, and at last past the roadsign into the city of Tours. Here Geoff was sitting in his car, grinning encouragement, thumbs up.

'Well done,' he said. 'I'm really impressed. *Now* will you have a day off? I want to see the châteaux of the Loire.'

Reaching the Loire at Tours marked the end of the first stage of my journey. With luck it might also mark an improvement in the weather, for over the years I have noticed that if you want to be sure of good weather in *la belle France*, you simply have to get to the Loire. Besides, it's a beautiful river.

The Loire is the longest river in France, running north and west from the Ardeche to pour into the Atlantic between Brittany and the Vendée, past the port of St Nazaire. It rises as a trickle down the slopes of the Gerbier de Jonc, a volcanic cone in the wilder Viverais, east of Le Puy, and actually flows south to begin with, getting to within fifty miles of the Mediterranean before it swings north, gaining strength all the way through the Nivernais and Berri, until it swings west at Orléans and flows majestically into Touraine and to where I now sat on the bridge at Tours, with the châteaux country to the east and the *châteaux-forts* country at my back, in Anjou. Geoff was right. Having walked this far, we ought to find some time to see the châteaux of the Loire.

The banks of the Loire, and the other great rivers of Touraine – the Cher, the Vienne and the Indre – are lined with châteaux. Further west, in the Plantagenet heartland of Anjou, the castles tend to be *châteaux-forts*, but here in the central valley, most of the châteaux date from the Renaissance period, although many of them stand on medieval foundations or still have parts of a former castle embedded in their structure. The great trick when visiting the châteaux country is to avoid château-glut by restricting your visits to a selected few. I explained this to Geoff over breakfast next morning, and we decided that since he had to depart for home that afternoon, we should make a whistle-stop car-tour to just three, Chenonceau, Amboise and Azay-le-Rideau, a small but fine and varied selection. The other alternative was to go on a literary pilgrimage, for this part of France is closely connected with Ronsard, the sixteenth-century poet who was born at the manor of La Poissonière on the Loir in 1524 – but his work can be read in books – we wanted to see art in stone.

Chenonceau is everyone's favourite château and, like so many of these 'Loire' châteaux, it stands not on the main river but on a tributary, the Cher. The present château was begun in 1513 by Thomas Bohier who was Intendant of Taxes to Charles VIII, and his two successors, Louis XII and François I. When Bohier died, François discovered that his Intendant had had his hand in the till, and seized the castle for the Crown in reparation. In 1547 Henri II gave Chenonceau to his beguiling mistress, Diane de Poitiers, but when Henri was killed in a tournament in 1559, his wife, Catherine de Medici forced Diane to exchange Chenonceau for her own rather less attractive castle of Chaumont.

Chenonceau is now in private hands, but supported by the Beaux Arts and open to visitors. It is a beautiful place, spanning the waters of the Cher and best seen in the morning, when the eastern sun fights up the finest façade. During the last war, the Cher marked the boundary between the Occupied and the Unoccupied Zones, and many escapees made their way down the long gallery, out of the German-held territory into the dubious safety of Vichy. The interior is almost as attractive as the breathtaking façades, with tapestries and paintings covering the walls. On this spring morning, pots of dwarf hyacinths were adding their heady scent to the air in the *grande gallerie* – delightful.

Amboise, six miles to the north of Chenonceau, is a medieval town on the south bank, and therefore best viewed from Negron on the far shore. There has been a castle here since Roman times, but the present buildings, which represent only about half of the original construction, date from the fifteenth and sixteenth centuries, when this castle was a favourite Royal residence and home to both Charles VIII and François I. Charles VIII – who had filled Amboise with the loot garnered during his Italian campaign against Naples – actually died here, of a brain contusion caused by hitting his head against a door lintel. His successor, François I, completed the castle and brought Leonardo da Vinci here, where he spent the last years of his life, died, and is buried. The castle of Amboise now belongs to the Count of Paris, Pretender to the Throne of France. On this sunny, Sunday morning, the little town that clusters below the castle walls was all that a French town should be: busy, pretty, full of shops, stalls and flowers, and well supplied with pleasant little restaurants, all open for business. We could have lingered here, but Napoleon's dictum, 'Ask of me anything but time', was always at the back of our minds, and we still had to see Azay.

Azay-le-Rideau, south-east of Tours, lies on the River Indre, my route for the next day. By now, however, since Geoff had a ferry to catch, I was looking anxiously at my watch.

'I know your driving is more like low flying, but even so, you're leaving it a bit late,' I told him. 'So we'll just have a quick peep at Azay, and then you must go.'

Like all the best castles, Azay-le-Rideau has a moat. Azay seems closer to a *château-fort* than most of the Loire châteaux, but that first impression is an illusion. The original *château-fort which* stood here was destroyed in 1418 by Charles, the Dauphin of France, and the present castle not built until the 1520s. The interior is therefore typically Renaissance and, even by modern standards, quite comfortable – full of furniture and tapestries, none of which we had time to see. Nevertheless, Balzac has described Azay as '. . this cut diamond set in the Indre and masked by flowers', so even a glimpse of the exterior is worth while.

'It's time to go,' said Geoff at last, braking to a halt beside the road. 'Now, are you sure you'll be all right?'

'I'll be fine. Don't worry about me,' I said, hauling my rucksack from the back seat. 'Just take it steady – French drivers are almost as daft as you are.'

'I'll see you in the Cévennes,' said Geoff, 'in about three weeks from now.'

I waited until Geoff had roared off out of sight towards the north. Then I shouldered my rucksack and began to walk east up the Indre Valley towards Cormery. After ten days on the trail, I had only about 520 miles still to do.

CHAPTER FOUR

ALONG THE INDRE

'One great fault of the English is the desire to discuss over and over again, the next day's route. I was driven out of doors by this kind of thing.'
T.J. Hogg

In my experience, the weather in France usually picks up once the traveller crosses the Loire, and so it was, briefly, on this occasion. I ambled across country to Cormery, across the green and fertile country of Touraine, under a high, blue sky, well supplied with fleecy clouds – driven like myself before a chilly north wind – through Azay-sur-Cher, past the beautiful priory at St-Jean-du-Grais, on a well-marked local footpath which was not a GR, and arrived at Cormery in the late afternoon.

Sunday afternoon at the popular Auberge du Mail at Cormery is still a busy time for the Grandson family. This little hotel is highly praised in all the best guides, and that evening it provided one of the most memorable meals of my journey, which cheered me up, because with Geoff's departure I felt just a little depressed. I knew this mood would soon pass because I have done many solitary trips and I know that I feel lonely only at the start. Then I slip into the way of it and start to move along at my own pace. Today, however, I was definitely down in the dumps, even though the trip was going more or less according to plan, the weather was looking up and I was leaving the chilly north for my favourite part of France, the Auvergne. To shake off my depression, I

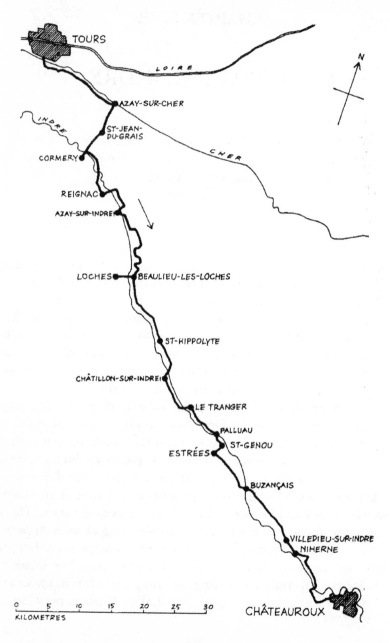

decided to ring home and find out what was happening back in Britain. This is easily done from any phone box and, apart from a gratifying amount of congratulations from my family on the fact that I had now reeled off the first 200 miles and was therefore on schedule, I also received the good news that Paul Traynor had decided to pack his rucksack and come south to join me. I have been on several memorable walks with Paul, once down the North Bucks Way, in hand-to-hand combat with the local farmers and, on another occasion, across the Pyrenees in late October. Then we met appalling weather and had to descend the north face of the mountains down snow-filled *couloirs,* and got out of the hills only by wading down a freezing river, an experience I would not be too eager to repeat. In any weather, Paul can hack it and, that apart, he is an entertaining, agreeable companion – and carries books.

Because of the weight problem I had been forced to leave all my books behind, but Paul never takes to the hills without two books which he considers essential. The first is the 1908 edition of Baden-Powell's *Scouting for Boys;* this contains useful advice on what to do if overwhelmed by the urge to commit what B-P describes as 'beastliness' (cold showers and upper-arm exercises are said to be efficacious), and how to escape a fate worse than death at the hands of the Matabele (learn skirt-dancing, whatever that may be), as well as many hints from the pioneering days of the great outdoors. Paul's second book is a well-thumbed 1912 edition of *Titles and Orders of Precedence of the European Nobility* which, he says, will tell you where to sit the Archbishop of Canterbury and a Grand Duchess of the Austro-Hungarian Empire, should they ever pitch up at your camp-fire for dinner one evening. We have spent many a storm-bound hour reading extracts from these two to each other, and the fact that Paul never actually turned up on this journey does not really matter. just anticipating his arrival cheered me up considerably at the time.

It is impossible to stay sad for long in the land south of the Loire, if only for historic reasons. Once upon a time, certainly until well into the Middle Ages, the River Loire divided France into two very different parts. To the north lay that part of old Gaul which was overrun by the Teutonic Franks when the Roman Empire disintegrated in the fifth century. To the south, the old *Provinca Romana*, now Provence, and what became the county of Toulouse was briefly occupied by the Visigoths before they moved on into Spain. Eventually the northern French came to dominate the whole country but, until the middle of the thirteenth century, France could be broadly divided into the aggressive expansionist north, and the romantic *laissez-faire* south, a division marked linguistically by the fact that in the north the word for 'yes' was '*ouil*' or '*oui*' and in the south '*oc*', hence 'Languedoc'. But the difference went much deeper. It was a question of attitude. To the north lived the hard-faced barons and ambitious courtiers who clustered round the court in Paris. Here, a man on the make might hope for advantage and position; in the south, or so it was said, the land offered nothing but wine and piety. Languedoc was the place where chivalry flourished, a country of fair ladies and gallant knights and, maybe, dragons. It was also the scene for the ferocious Albigensian Crusade, but on the whole, the southern folk were lighthearted, and happy with their lot. There is the story of a troubadour from Languedoc who stopped his horse on a bridge over the Loire and contemplated his future. To the north lay royal patronage and wealth, to the south only song, sun and poetry. The troubadour wisely turned his back on fame and fortune and rode south, on a journey so delightful that even his horse sang. I'd like to have heard that.

Languedoc is still the romantic half of France, whatever the claims of not-always *gay Paree*. Here, south of the Loire, the sun shines, the Mediterranean is blue, the rivers are rushing, sparkling torrents, the towns stand out in golden stone, roofed in red, their streets picked out with scarlet geraniums which glow in the window boxes. Here you find the great castles, the finest cathedrals and the little walled towns, the *bastides* of the Dordogne or Quercy. It is a land of wine, sun, song and history, and you would have to be very short on soul not to find Languedoc delightful, even though the old sprawling land of Oc has shrunk to a single province south of the Montagne Noire.

History has marked France more deeply than most other lands, and for those who take the trouble to look beneath the surface, the scars and landmarks still remain. At the start of the last thousand years the then Kings of France, the Capets, were little more than *primus inter pares*, encircled by powerful barons, and much of French history is an account of the rulers' efforts to expand their rule over the whole country, far beyond their personal domain in the Ile de France; to settle the hash of their rivals and cousins, the Plantagenet Kings of England; and lastly to obtain secure and recognised frontiers for their country. All this took time and the task was finally completed only in 1945, when the disputed provinces of Alsace and Lorraine were firmly and, one hopes, finally reattached to France. In the process the Kings of France were deposed, but their relics remain – most notably here, along the river country of the Loire, in the old fortified towns and castles which speckle the land as reminders of those endless conflicts.

To the west of where I now lay dozing on my bed at Cormery, lay the ancient country of Anjou, one of the great fiefs of the Kingdom of France, ruled in the early Middle Ages by a turbulent family who ignored the King's edicts and fought with their traditional rivals, the Counts of Blois, for the lordship of Touraine. The greatest of these Counts of Anjou was Count Geoffrey, who ruled in Angers from 1113 to 1151. He held Anjou from the King of France, the country of Maine from the Duke of Normandy and, he maintained, the lordship of Touraine, which almost everyone else felt to be a fief of the country of Blois. Count

Geoffrey did homage to his rival of Blois with the greatest reluctance and rebelled whenever he could, with the result that the Touraine is studded with great *châteaux-forts*. Most of these were built, or at least commenced, by Count Geoffrey or his immediate forebears. Among these they could number the Devil, so the Counts of Anjou were often referred to as 'The Devil's Brood'.

In the twelfth century the story of the Devil's Brood was widely known and almost as widely believed. Apparently, at some time in the not too distant past, a Count of Anjou had gone on a journey, and returned after a long time accompanied by a beautiful lady whom he then married. The union seemed happy enough and produced four children, but two things about his lady bothered the Count and his Court. Firstly, the lady had no relatives, which was curious in an age when the nobility were often related, and secondly, she refused to attend Mass, which was a scandal. She would, in fact, attend the early part of the service but would always leave as soon as the bell tinkled for the Elevation of the Host, when the bread and wine became the Body and Blood of Christ. Finally, to prevent this disrespect, the Count ordered two of his heaviest knights to get behind her and stand on the hem of her cloak. This they did, but with terrible consequences. The bell tinkled, the lady turned to depart, found herself checked, screamed, then tore herself loose and, seizing two of her children, flew out of the chapel window never to be seen again. She was, the Count confessed, Melusine, the Devil's own daughter. From the two children she left behind, all the Counts of Anjou, many later Kings of England and – now I come to think of it – our present Royal Family, are directly descended.

Count Geoffrey, father of Henry II of England, had one other notable characteristic. Like every medieval lord he was passionately fond of hunting and hawking, so, to improve the ground cover, he always carried a slip of gorse or broom in his cap, and would plant it wherever he thought it might take root.

This peasant habit was considered so unusual for a great lord that it earned Count Geoffrey the nickname Plantagenet – or the broom planter (broom in French is *genet)*, and so arose one of history's famous surnames. The Plantagenets have gone but the broom remains, flowering on the hillsides of Anjou and Touraine, and some of the locals still cut off the green branches and bind them to staffs to make *balais* – or brooms.

At Tours I had left the GR36, which rambled on due south across Poitou, and turned south-east on a newer footpath, the GR46, which is shown only on the newer IGN maps and is still without a *topo-guide*. This left me to rely on waymarks for most of the next week, but the route is not difficult to follow. It stays close to the winding Indre all the way south-east to Châteauroux and beyond, out of Touraine, across the old dukedom of Berri and into the Limousin.

Next morning I was up by seven-thirty and on the road by half past eight, stopping briefly to buy a bag of those macaroons for which Cormery is famous and to inspect the Church of Notre-Dame-du-Fougery and the crumbling *Lanterne des Morts* in the churchyard opposite. These pencil-shaped towers, like small minarets, are fairly rare and usually in ruins, although there is a fine intact example at Sariat in the Dordogne. No one seems certain about their origin or exactly what they are for, but they were probably erected as lantern towers to indicate the presence of an open grave, a plague victim or – and there are recent examples of this – to mark the death of a Head of State. The lantern in Sarlat was lit when De Gaulle died.

Cormery grew up around the abbey founded by a priest from the Cathedral of St Martin in Tours about 791, so it is a very old town, with various remnants of fortification – notably one massive tower, the Tour St Paul, which still dominates the rooftops and the surrounding fields. The Indre countryside is fairly flat, the river now in full flood was slow and winding, so it was a fairly easy morning, even with my heavy pack, first to Reignac and Azay-sur-Indre, which has a huge, square *château-fort* and a mill astride the river. The castle here once belonged to the quixotic Maquis de la Fayette, who fought for the United States during the American Revolution. I was going well and feeling fresh, so getting to Azay, eight miles from Cormery, took just over two hours. A further nine miles along the GR46 on the north bank of the river, with the sun now bursting out to encourage the swallows, went somewhat slower but brought me to Beaulieu-les-Loches where, my legs aching, I fell into a small bar full of locals just finishing their lunch. One old man was already asleep over his coffee, while one of the younger lads was sitting at the bar in his vest while the bar-lady ironed his shirt.

Beaulieu contains the ruins of an abbey where Fulk Nerra, one of the more violent of the Devil's Brood, lies buried. Fulk founded the abbey in 1004 in an attempt to expiate his numerous crimes, but his offer was rejected. A tornado tore the abbey apart and it had to be rebuilt after his death. Fulk was noted for his wickedness and, while on pilgrimage to Jerusalem, he again attempted to ensure his soul's survival and obtained a piece of the Holy Sepulchre by biting off a lump of stone from it with his teeth.

Half an hour in the *café* braced me for the last lap across the river into Loches, but when I got there I discovered that my hotel, the Logis Lucchotel, actually lay a mile out of town at the top of a hill – a long, slow plod on that hot afternoon, when I was already very tired.

The climb was worth it, for the views from the hotel across the rooftops of Loches and the Indre valley are quite superb. Loches is a black and white Touraine town, all dark-tiled roofs above white-gold walls sparkling in the sun, set in a circle of fresh green woods and fields, all dominated by the great grim keep of Fulk Nerra's castle. Built in the eleventh century, it remained in use until as recently as 1926.

Having dumped boots and pack, I walked slowly back into town for a closer look at the castle. This subjected my legs to an unwelcome dose of stairs, because the castle of Loches is an up-and-down place, of deep *oubliettes* and one tall *donjon* or tower. Those with a head for heights can climb to the top of this tower from where, on a small, windy, vertiginous platform, they can enjoy great views over the surrounding countryside.

I like castles, and the one at Loches is a particularly fine example of the medieval *château-fort*. Loches has always been a fortress city, and the scene of countless sieges down the centuries, most notably when Richard Coeur de Lion strove with Phillipe-Augustus for the mastery of France. In the later Middle Ages, Loches became a State Prison and remained as such until the present century, and so a tour of the castle includes a visit to the cells and the torture chamber. Nearly all the fortresses which were turned into prisons contain a torture chamber because, until the time of Louis XV, torture formed part of the judicial examining process; indeed the unsavoury place was often euphemistically called The Question Room. Even today the brochure on the castle of Loches gives a chilly description of what went on there. 'In order to make prisoners confess, various forms of torture could be used; that was the Ordinary Question. If the prisoner had committed a crime or a misdemeanour which was considered important enough, he was tortured again; that was the Extraordinary Question.' The Question Room at Loches, which still contains the iron bars and chains to which the prisoners were secured for The Question, was installed at the orders of Charles VII about 1450.

The first of the famous cages of Loches, where those inside could neither sit nor stand nor lie down, was introduced by his successor, Louis XI, as a torment for his traitorous counsellor, the Cardinal Balue, who had betrayed Louis to his enemy, the Duke of Burgundy. The cage was certainly installed at Loches, for the cost appears in the Royal accounts, but there is no evidence that the Cardinal was actually placed in it, and he survived eleven years' imprisonment at Loches before he was finally freed. Other prisoners held in Loches included the unlucky Ludovico Sforza, the Duke of Milan, who was held here from 1500 to 1508. When he was finally released from his dank, chilly cell, he died of joy on seeing the sun again. The castle contains the rooms where Joan of Arc came to collect the Dauphin for his coronation at Reims, and the tomb of the beautiful Agnes Sorel, mistress of Charles VII, as well as other interesting relics. I spent a happy couple of hours at the castle and in the Church of St Ours, before ambling back through Loches to my hotel.

Dinner that night at the Lucchotel made the perfect end to a good day, looking down over the lights of the town from a dining room decorated with Impressionist prints, while an attentive staff took me under their wing, serving *saumon et barbue marines au citron et au poivre vert*, with a half-bottle of Vouvray, the local wine. I finished off with a selection of local cheeses from St Maur and Valençay. The high standard of service offered in French hotels, often by a very young staff, never ceases to amaze me, especially when I contrast it with the lackadaisical or downright indifferent treatment commonly experienced at home. Granted, hotel or restaurant work is a highly regarded craft in France, while the British have never been able to discriminate between good service, which reflects credit on the performer, and servility, which simply embarrasses all concerned. It has also, I suspect, something to do with personal pride. The French take personal pride in what they do and so command the respect of their clients. The British tend to think that serving others is undeniably degrading and compensate for their shame by doing it, if at all, in the most amateur fashion and with as little goodwill as possible. I think that is both a pity, and wrong. I went off to bed here in a very good mood and slept well, to awake feeling more than ready for another good long day. I had intended to storm down the Indre valley as quickly as possible, maybe gaining a day on my schedule, but the towns lie just fifteen miles apart, which is the perfect daily distance, and I felt no particular urge to exceed this.

I left Loches early, getting on the road before nine. Following the GR46 waymarks to St-Hippolyte, I came out on to the road just in front of a long convoy of horse-drawn gypsy caravans, a picturesque sight at first, the vans crammed with smiling children. However, when I took a photograph, the smiles were switched off and one of the children hurled a boot at me. The GR46 path through the fields was then swallowed by the flooding Indre, so minor roads took me through a succession of small Indre villages, each with its church, their strangely bulbous black towers rearing up above the rooftops like space rockets. I took an hour off in one of these to rest my feet and shelter yet again from the rain which had swept back in force. But during that long, wet afternoon, I ticked off another province, passing from Touraine into the dukedom of Berri at about four o'clock in the afternoon.

Berri was one of the great dukedoms of France, which rose to considerable splendour during the latter half of the Hundred Years War, when it was ruled by Jean, Duc de Berri, who lived to the then great age of seventy-six and preferred, if possible, to stay away from both the conflicts between his house and the Plantagenets, and the brawls between the rival French factions of Burgundy and Armagnac. The Duke was much more interested in women. 'The more the merrier and never tell the truth', is one of his recorded maxims. He built wonderfully, filling his duchy with magnificent castles, full of pictures and sculpture and tapestry. He also loved the chase and is said to have kept no less than 1,500 dogs, but his contemporaries were rather more amazed that his library contained no less than eighty books, among them the beautiful, illustrated work known as *Les Très Riches Heures.*

87

Duke Jean was far less ambitious than his brother Philip the Bold, Duke of Burgundy, and far too lazy to extend his demesne beyond the great inheritance ceded to him by his father, Jean le Bon, which comprised the Limousin, Berri, and much of the Auvergne. Duke Jean still saw his fair share of strife, and he eventually fell out with his nephew Charles VI, and then signed a treaty with the English which led to his ruin. His capital, Bourges, was besieged by the French Army in 1412, and after it fell most of his power and possessions were stripped away. The Dauphin Charles took possession of Berri in 1417 and ruled there while the armies of Henry V and Henry VI ravaged France in the years after Agincourt. Indeed, the English often called him, contemptuously, 'The King of Bourges', at least until Joan of Arc rode into Chinon in 1429.

I can think of worse places to live and rule in than this delightful county of Berri, a very *douce* part of France. The writer, Alain Fournier, said that Berri was '. . really the great region of France, and one that strangers can't talk about much, because its general appearance doesn't say anything. You have to know it.' Having walked across it, that seems to me to be absolutely true. Berri is simply beautiful, and beautiful in a simple way.

Modern Berri lies north of the River Creuse, and south of the Loire, where it curves in from the Touraine, between Bourges and the two southern-most cities of Montluçon and Châteauroux. These two lie at the south-eastern end of the Indre valley some thirty miles away, and it was towards the latter which my steps were now directed. Meanwhile, it was raining, my pack was dragging on my back and I felt that I had done enough, at least for one day. I climbed the hill into the jumbled streets of Châtillon-sur-Indre, past the great Church of Notre Dame and on to the Auberge de la Tour in the Route du Blanc.

The auberge doors were firmly shut, a considerable disappointment to a wet, tired walker, but as I was plodding wearily away down the street in search of a bar, there came a clattering on the cobbles behind and one of the maids came rushing after me.

'Monsieur, are you the English walker?'

'I am.'

'Well, then . . .' she gestured to the now open door of the hotel, '*Je vous en prie . . . .*'

Monsieur and Madame Nicolas, who were enjoying a quiet afternoon in their sitting room, were hospitality itself. A stiff drink arrived to take the chill away, with the suggestion that if I cared to give Madame all my clothes, which were clearly in need of a wash, I could have them back by morning. This seemed a very good idea. I also took the opportunity to ring ahead to the Auvergne and see how the weather was in the mountains of the Massif Central. Some of the rain which had been scourging me for the past two weeks must have been falling as snow on the high peaks further south, a view that the tourist office in Le Mont-Dore was only too pleased to confirm. Yes, they had snow, the skiing was still good, but if I wanted to enjoy the snow I should hurry. Enjoying the snow was the least of my ambitions, but that particular problem still lay ten days away, and a lot could happen before I had to face it. Putting that aside for the moment, I settled down for a chat with Monsieur Nicolas, who was very enthusiastic, even envious, about my journey. His life was spent chained to his bar and therefore dominated by the whims of his clients and the demands of his staff.

'But then you have the time – and you are at the age to enjoy a little leisure. But, of course, fifty is a wonderful age for a man.'

'Really?' Since I was exhausting myself every day and have yet to make my fortune, I felt a little doubtful about the benefits of my half-century, but Monsieur Nicolas was certain that this was my Golden Age.

'Oh, but yes.' He looked around nervously before continuing. 'Listen. When you are fifty and you meet a beautiful woman well, if she says "Yes", you are flattered . . . and if she says "No", well, you are relieved . . . eh?'

He had a point there.

Next day began with a bonus, for Monsieur Nicolas, having business to do in Buzançais, offered to carry my rucksack forward to the next hotel, an offer I accepted with alacrity. Once again lightly loaded, I thanked Madame Nicolas for my now pristine clothing and set off along the right bank of the Indre for Le Tranger. The rain had stopped and it was a fairly hot, sleepy sort of day, when the bees came out to buzz around the flowers, and I saw my first rain-battered group of tulips, another sign of spring . . . and so to pretty Palluau. Monsieur Nicolas had recommended following the north bank whatever the GR46 path did, because, he said, the places on the north bank are more interesting. He was right. Palluau runs along a ridge above the river, and is dominated by a castle begun by Fulk Rechin, the father of Fulk Nerra. The chancel of the castle chapel is decorated with remarkable Renaissance frescoes, and from the tower there are magnificent views all along the valley. I could have spent a lot more time in Palluau, but as it was still only niidday, I slipped out of town to the clanging of the Angelus and crossed the river, strolling down a long tree-lined avenue to St-Genou and up the hill to Estrées, past yet another crumbling *Lanterne des Morts*. Here, for no good reason, my right leg started to hurt and went on hurting until my pace was reduced to a hobble. That was the way it went for the first couple of weeks, with muscle after muscle taking it in turn to protest.

Apart from that there were no particular problems, though even at the end of the journey my feet and legs were still very tired by the end of a twenty-mile stage. Eventually I came to accept that after that distance in a day, my eyes would start to water a bit and that there was nothing to do but put up with it. I could delay the discomfort for a while by stopping from time to time for a rest, a beer or a coffee and slackening off the bootlaces to give my feet a rest. I tried this in a roadside café near Buzançais, where the bar carried a notice, '*Trop de repose na jamais fait mourir personne*' – 'Too much rest never killed anybody' – a sentiment with which I entirely agreed. I got very attached to these little rest-stops; fifteen minutes with my feet up and a browse through the local paper helped to break up days which were otherwise devoted to hard slog. Anywhere abroad, the local paper is always worth a look and that for Buzançais had a fine selection of small advertisements, *les petites annonces*. '*Le délégué de la Club du Yorkshire est à Vote disposition*', confused me for a while, until I realised this was about terriers, not cricket. More intriguing still was one by '*une belle blonde, à top-look, indep, charme, vick-ing, gaie et vibrante, recontre monsieur, pour tendre complicité*'. Well, well, but what was '*vick-ing*' I wondered.

On this particular day, when the sun refused for once to share the space with rain, I limped painfully on into Buzançais and was very glad indeed to reach my night-stop at the Hôtel Croissant where, after the usual warm greeting, a chat with the owner about my route and my feet, and a swift photo-session with the local paper, I crawled upstairs to get organised.

The great trick on a long journey is to establish a routine quickly. This is where the lone traveller is at an advantage, for he has no one to please but himself. My routine, which I slipped into after a couple of days and maintained to the end, was to arrive at my night-stop, down a beer and then lug my rucksack upstairs to my room where, after a shower or a bath, I would wash out my shirt, socks and underwear and hang them up to dry on the radiators. In most of these small hotels the heating did not come on until seven o'clock, but although the socks usually needed a day or two to dry completely, the other garments were normally ready to put on in the morning. This went wrong from time to time, giving me the choice of a dirty shirt or a wet one, but on the whole I coped well enough and managed not to lose anything, which was a good thing, as my one-on, one-off choice of garment did not allow me to festoon the world with my underwear, as I usually do. Some years ago, cycling to Compostela, I stopped for a coffee after an hour or so on the road and, putting my hand in my pocket, found I had taken the hotel room-key with me. I was sitting on my bike, holding the key and wondering what to do, when a car screeched to a stop alongside and the hotel-lady leaned out to offer me my underpants which she had found in the bathroom. I handed over the key, she handed over my underpants and drove off. When I turned towards the café, I found a small crowd in the window who had watched this exchange with considerable amusement . . . and didn't believe a word of my explanation.

Having washed my clothes, I would repack the rucksack, write up my notes and go out to see the town or whatever sights lay within limping distance, followed by dinner and an early night. In the morning I had breakfast in my room whenever possible, moving about stiffly until the leg muscles warmed up. I tried to get on the trail before nine, following the well-proven rule that an hour's walking in the morning is much easier than an hour in the afternoon. My aim was to get the bulk of my daily distance covered by lunchtime, when I might, if I had succeeded in this aim and a suitable restaurant presented itself, reward myself with lunch. By the early evening, say between four and five, I would arrive at the hotel, which I had pre-booked the day before or even earlier, when the process would repeat itself. This 'old maid's' approach kept me plodding on across France.

In the Hôtel Croissant I was met by the entire Desroches family, from Michel and Christine down to Dolly the poodle. Dolly the poodle promptly attacked my boots and had a fight with the laces. Michel had clearly been well briefed that morning by Monsieur Nicolas, because he had the Armagnac out before I was halfway through the front door and said he would arrange for someone to take my pack down the road to Châteauroux the following day. That decided (and any day without the pack was worth looking forward to), I settled down to a pleasant evening, picking my way through the menu . . . *feuillette descargots à la crème d'ail,* followed by *foie de veau au miel et vinaigre de framboise* – quite delicious, and topped off with *chèvre blanc en toast,* or 'goat on toast' as the Ferrets call it. After that I went out again, to take my *digestif* in a café further up the hill.

Buzançais is a pretty little place, once contained within medieval walls and now a touring centre for the wetlands of the Brenne, which lie a little distance to the south, a region of lakes and a paradise for fishermen and birdwatchers. The Brenne is one of those areas which the tourist rushing through France by car is almost sure to miss. I have been there only once, on my bicycle, but I remember it as a green, enchanted land, full of great castles – like Romfort near Ciran, or the one at Bouchet near Rosney – of Romanesque churches and dovecotes and small, golden-stone villages. Most of all, the Brenne is a paradise for birds, especially for waterfowl, attracted here in their tens of thousands by the wetlands south of Mézières. From a café table in Buzançais I watched the sun sink into a golden mist above the Brenne, while hundreds of ducks plugged their way towards it through the evening sky.

The Croissant is one of those family-run French hotels where the family has been extended to cover the guests, who come in to take Dolly for her walk or join the children before the television. The same locals drop in for a drink every evening, drooping over their wine glasses like chess players. To all these I was an object of interested concern, especially from Christine, who was quite sure I must be a bachelor, and no denial or photograph would convince her otherwise.

'No French woman would let her husband go off on his own like this for weeks on end . . . you could get into all sorts of trouble.' I never had the chance to get into that sort of trouble. The other customers were mostly interested in the technical stuff; how many kilometres I did each day, where I had started, where I was going. In spite of the extent and excellence of the GR trails or maybe because of them – I rarely met other long-distance walkers in France, and most people seemed to find my project astonishing if not, in fact, crazy. I bow to no one in my respect for the French, but after a few weeks, I did get more than a little tired of answering the same questions, to yet another set of raised eyebrows.

Pleasant evenings are often followed by chill dawns. I awoke to the usual thin rain, had breakfast with the children, fed sugared almonds to Dolly and then helped another new friend, the driver who was taking my luggage on to Châteauroux, to load my rucksack into his van. Then I set off to plod south to Châteauroux, a flat, easy, seventeen-mile hike which I ripped off in four hours, storming past the decayed château at Villedieu-sur-Indre and the *Maquis* Cross-of-Lorraine memorial at Niherne, to cross the river bridge over the Indre and arrive in the town just in time for a late lunch. I spent the afternoon dodging from doorway to doorway in the rain, while prowling the bookshops of the town in fruitless search for a copy of the GR4 (Aubusson to St Flour) *topo-guide*, which was long out of print, although in the Tourist Office I found a trial *topo-guide* to the GR46, the green-backed edition produced as a trial run before the proper *topo-guide* is eventually published by the FFRP-CNSGR. Had I obtained this in Tours at the start of the GR46, it would have been quite useful. I began to worry just a little about the lack of information available on walking through the Auvergne and the ever-more-weighty collection of cards and leaflets now resting in my rucksack.

Châteauroux is a large town by French provincial standards, with a population of about 50,000. The capital of lower Berri, it is a centre for touring the George Sand country, which lies further to the south-east between Châteauroux and my next destination, La Châtre. The big attractions here for the history buff are the splendid fifteenth-century Château Raoul – right in the middle of the town, which now contains the Préfecture – and the Musée Bertrand, once the home of the loyal and long-suffering General Bertrand, Napoleon's Chief-of-Staff, which contains all manner of Napoleonic memorabilia and is a good place to lurk on a wet afternoon. I had covered only sixty miles from Tours in the last four days. I was still on both the GR46 and the River Indre, and so without the lift that comes from definite progress, but I felt that at last, day by day, I was moving into higher, wilder country. I had now been walking for two full weeks and, if my physical condition was not obviously better, neither was it any worse. I had crossed Normandy and Maine and Touraine, and before long I would leave Berri behind and be in the Limousin, the last lap before I reached the Auvergne. There I would turn south to cross the Massif Central, and remain in the hills all the way south to the sea. Looking in the niirror that morning, I even discovered the beginnings of a tan. I hurried downstairs, swallowed my croissant and coffee, and sped out of town, through the forest of Châteauroux. I had a long way to go that day before I arrived at La Châtre, nearly thirty miles away in the green country of the Limousin.

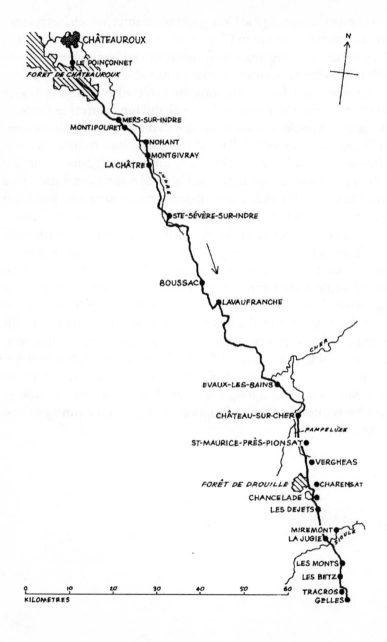

CHÂTEAUROUX
LE POINÇONNET
FORÊT DE CHÂTEAUROUX
MERS-SUR-INDRE
MONTIPOURET
NOHANT
MONTGIVRAY
LA CHÂTRE
INDRE
STE-SÉVÈRE-SUR-INDRE
BOUSSAC
LAVAUFRANCHE
CHER
EVAUX-LES-BAINS
CHÂTEAU-SUR-CHER
PAMPELUXE
ST-MAURICE-PRÈS-PIONSAT
VERGHEAS
FORÊT DE DROUILLE
CHARENSAT
CHANCELADE
LES DEJETS
MIREMONT
LA JUGIE
SIOULE
LES MONTS
LES BETZ
TRACROS
GELLES

N

0 10 20 30 40 50 60
KILOMÈTRES

CHAPTER FIVE

BERRI AND THE LIMOUSIN

'There is no point in setting out for
anywhere one seems certain to reach.'
Bill Tilman

Châteauuroux is a large town, and it seems even larger when one has to walk out of it. I had to walk four miles south, just to clear the outer suburbs before angling off on a narrow ride through the Forêt de Châteauuroux towards La Châtre, keeping as close as possible to the direct line ruled in on my map. I avoided the major roads and hit the GR46 only occasionally as it wandered to and fro across the woods. I picked it up again at Le Poinçonnet, on the southern edge of the forest. Out here the countryside was empty and I walked for three hours through the forest, and met not a soul, saw not even a car.

As usual, it was raining. This particular forest ride was dedicated – for no good reason I could think of – to Louis XIII, one of France's less distinguished monarchs, who did manage to drive the Spanish back across the Pyrenees out of Roussillon, but otherwise spent most of his life under the dominance of Cardinal Richelieu. These communal forests are a relic from pre-Revolutionary days, and were taken over by the people when the local lord was either led to the guillotine or forced into exile. They remain today more or less intact for the benefit and recreation of the local people, who often enjoy communal rights to extract timber or hunt the deer for example, just as the *seigneurs* did in days gone by. They are also marvellous habitats for wildlife.

Birds abound and the wild boar, so long extinguished in Britain, is common in the forests of France.

On the way through the wood, I passed a large monument to the *Maquis*, the Resistance fighters of Berri, and shortly after this arrived first at Mers-sur-Indre, a little hamlet, and then, after climbing a hill, at Montipouret. It was getting towards midday and I was in urgent need of lunch. I had a very strange conversation with a man I met in the main street of Montipouret, who insisted on keeping his distance and circling me cautiously while we conversed. Yes, he said, there was a restaurant up the hill by the church, but it would probably be closed unless I hurried. When I hurried off, he followed on the far side of the road, which was a touch unnerving.

'Are you a parachutist?' he asked at last, coming alongside, but still staying on the far side of the road.

'A what? – of course not! I'm walking through France, that's all.'

'Then why are you wearing a parachute?' he asked triumphantly, pointing to my rucksack. That explained it; the man was clearly a lunatic.

He trailed behind me, muttering, and remained completely unconvinced that it was simply a *sac-à-dos*, but I was too tired to argue with the village idiot. He followed me into the café where, although lunch was over, a nice woman agreed to make me an omelette, and he sat at the bar watching me suspiciously until I paid up and left.

'He's a parachutist,' he said to her as I walked out of the door.

This southern part of Berri, and the top left-hand corner of the Limousin, hints at the approaching Auvergne. I could see that much, simply by glancing at the map, for the contour lines were beginning to multiply and grow ever closer together, which indicated a far more interesting, if more testing, terrain. Apart from waymarks, maps, and compass, I now took direction from the sun, which was making some effort to shine, and from the fighters of the French Air Force. If I had the sun more or less on my left cheek, and the Mirages screaming past across my right shoulder, heading for low-level flying around the mountains of the Massif, I knew I was heading in the right direction, even if I was well off-track. Much of the art of cross-country navigation is bound up with little things, with minor indications – the direction of a stream, the prevailing wind, the tailings left by melting snow: all these can help the walker find the way.

This southern part of Berri, around La Châtre, is the land of George Sand, the nineteenth-century novelist. Since writing is my profession, I thought I would veer left to Nohant and look at her home, the Château de Nohant, a little south of the village. The young Aurore Dupin – which seems a perfectly good writer's name to me – came to live with her grandmother in Nohant after the death of her father. She spent most of her childhood there, married Baron Dudevent, had two children, and left him to live in Paris with her lover, Jules Sandeau. There she took up a way of life that might be considered a little extreme even today, cropping her hair, smoking, taking numerous lovers, flouting every convention of a very conventional society.

Her first book, written under the pseudonym of George Sand, was published in 1832, when she was twenty-eight. From then on she wrote incessantly, setting many of her books in her homeland of the Berri, and in particular in the valley of the Creuse. In *Laura,* she wrote that the Creuse was ' ... *peut-être la plus belle rivière du monde, au mois d'Avril'.* I passed the Creuse in April and it looked pretty dreary in the rain. Sand returned to Nohant in the 1860s and died there in 1876. George Sand's work may be little-known today, when she is chiefly remembered for her affair with Chopin, but she was a lion – or lioness – in the literary world of her time, and her output was prodigious. She wrote over sixty books and twenty-five plays, while her personal correspondence was amazing; her collected correspondence contains over thirteen thousand letters. When she died, all the *literati* flocked to the funeral and Victor Hugo delivered the eulogy.

The eighteenth-century château at Nohant – where Sand entertained Chopin, Liszt, Balzac, Dumas, Flaubert, and others of her circle – is preserved as a museum and her study is very much as she left it. Apart from her desk and a well-stocked library, the château contains a theatre where her children entertained the guests with marionette shows. Her grave occupies the centre of the family cemetery in the park, a green and pleasant place to end up after a life which was never exactly tranquil. I was shown all this by the *guardien*, who told me I was the first visitor they had had that year.

I had diverted into Nohant from a *variente* of the GR46 and to get back on to my direct road for La Châtre I had to cross the D943 and drop south again through Montgivray. Arriving in La Châtre in the early evening, I limped down to my hotel, the very pleasant, rather modern Les Tanneries where, boots off and sprawled on my bed, I watched my feet swell up. I had walked about thirty miles that day and once again I'd overdone it. I actually caught myself groaning, and limped in to dinner that evening in my socks which, since it was Saturday and the restaurant was full of smart young people, caused something of a stir.

After dinner my feet and spirits had recovered enough for a tour of the town, which is set on a hill overlooking the Indre, in the part known to George Sand as the *Vallie Noire*. There was a marching camp here in Roman times, hence the name La Châtre, from *castra*, a camp, and the town is that now familiar but still pleasing maze of medieval streets, where small shops and stalls jostle for space along the pavements, and hump-backed, packhorse bridges span the narrowing river. I spent an enjoyable hour here, and was sound asleep long before midnight.

One small sign of growing fitness is a quick recovery process. In six weeks I never became so fit that a twenty-five mile bash with the rucksack became easy, but with nearly 300 miles completed, I was fit enough to do the whole thing again on the following day. I left La Châtre early in the morning, marching hard for Boussac under a bright sky, on a wandering route that had me in Ste Sévère just in time for lunch at Alain Blanchet's beautiful Hôtel l'Ecu de France, where the oak-beamed dining room was bright with brass and fresh flowers. Ste Sévère is an old town, and the saint herself was the abbess at the nearby Merovingian nunnery. I spent my lunch browsing over a booklet on local history, which included tales of the time when Constable Duguesclin arrived to chase away the English who had occupied the castle during the Hundred Years War, the fact that George Sand set her novel *Mauprat* in the town and, of more recent date, that this was the place featured by Jacques Tati in his film *Jour de Fête*. Ste Sévère is another agreeable little town, quite busy even on a Sunday, but I could not linger too long as Boussac was still a long way away, and the terrain was becoming ever more jumbled.

I left Ste Sévère in a good mood, only to run into my daily dose of bad luck, in the shape of a group of French ramblers out walking on the GR46. They took me in hand, got lost, led me in the wrong direction, and finally arrived back at their cars at six o'clock, at which point they departed. This was the first group of French walkers I had seen since the second day in the Suisse-Normande, and as I flogged on across France, this absence of walkers continued to surprise me. Here we have a country with nearly 30,000 miles of long-distance trail, the FFRP which claims tens of thousands of adherents, a number of excellent clubs or organisations like the *Club Vosgian*, ABRI in Brittany, *Randonnée Pyrénéan* for the Pyrenees, Chamina for the Massif Central, and many others in every part of France, yet the number of people actually setting boot to footpath seemed minimal. When they walked at all, they walked only on a daily basis. Perhaps the

French are keener on cycling than on walking, for I have never lacked for company on any cycle tour in France – indeed at weekends even the minor French roads can become positively crowded with *vélos,* their riders all tricked out in the latest clothing, however short and leisurely the ride.

The French are like that; they may not be able to do it but they like to look the part. I well remember seeing a French tennis player arrive on the court in glittering whites, complete with wrist-bands, choose from half a dozen mckets, instruct the *petite-amie* to get ready – and serve underarm. The problem now, in the late afternoon, was that I had walked off my map and had no idea where I was. Marching south on a compass bearing, it took me until well after dark to retrace my steps to the GR46 and stumble wearily into my hotel at Boussac, on the Creuse. I had made it out of Berri and into Limousin – another province dealt with, another long day's march at my back.

I like the Limousin. It is one of those sprawling, little-visited parts of France which, though surrounded by popular places – Périgord, the Loire – still remains somehow undiscovered. It is, therefore, just perfect for the wandering Francophile. It is said to produce the prettiest girls in France, which may well be true, although Jean Giraudoux said that the Limousin has bred more popes and fewer lovers than anywhere else on earth, which would seem to contradict this. It can certainly lay claim to some beautiful scenery and many fine towns, not least Limoges, the ancient capital of this green and pleasant province. Apart from fine porcelain, Limoges was the place where those French generals who had made a mess of their campaigns on the Western Front were sent into early retirement, so Limoges has provided France with a tactful verb, *limoger,* 'to be sacked, or made redundant'. Somehow 'Cheltenhamer' does not work in quite the same way.

The Limousin presently consists of three varied *départements,* of which the one I was crossing – the Creuse – contains most of the medieval country of La Marche. To the east lies the high, wet plateau of the Millevaches – forested, seamed with little watercourses, full of cattle, surprisingly barren, but to my taste quite delightful. To the north-west the Limousin is more hilly, speckled with range after range of small hills that may try to be mountains but just fail to make it. The Marche, the most northern part, just south of the Champagne-Berrichon, divides the lush country of the Loire from the rugged country of the Auvergne, and, as is proper on a march, the region is well supplied with castles and fortified towns, of which Boussac is a splendid example. Boussac lies on the Petite-Creuse, a tributary of the main river which, like so many French rivers, gives its name to the local *département.*

Boussac straddles the little river (which means that I had at last left the Indre behind) and, being a frontier town, contains a very fine fifteenth-century castle where the main gateway bears the blazon of Jean de Brosse, Lord of Boussac in the fifteenth century, who rode with Joan of Arc to lift the siege of Orléans. I strolled about the streets until well after ten the next day, letting the air warm up, and about mid-morning embarked on a new footpath, the GR41, which would carry me south into the Auvergne. Once again, I felt I was getting somewhere, and I needed that encouragement because my feet were now becoming very painful and reducing my pace to a slow limp.

Two hours' walking brought me to Lavaufranche, a little place notable only because it contains a well-preserved castle or *commanderie,* built in the twelfth century by the Knights of St John, the *Hospitaliers.* The Military Orders built similar *commanderies* all over western Europe during the time of the Crusades, places where men could be recruited and trained, and where money could be collected to sustain the Orders' efforts in the Holy Land. Some examples, like La Couvertoirade further south, are very large, but this one at Lavaufranche is more typical. A fortified manor rather than a proper castle, it is in an excellent state of preservation. Three floors are open to view, but my legs balked at the stairs, so I sat down for a rest on the wall outside and fed barley-sugar to some ponies until my supply ran out.

A little south of Lavaufranche, wandering along, I found an even less common and more curious sight, a line of scarecrows up in the trees along the road, among branches decorated with scraps of coloured cloth. What these were for I could not discover because, as usual, there was not a soul in sight. They may just have been there to keep the birds off the fruit blossom, or for some more mystic purpose, for the Limousin is a land of fairies, witches, saints, sorcerers and hobgoblins – or at least it was, and in these country districts people prefer to keep their guard up. Once every seven years, the people of the Creuse placate and invoke the aid of their local saints, St Martial, Ste Valérie, St Eloi and St Etienne, by holding pageants and processions, *les ostension*, which are not unlike the Breton *pardons,* a time when relics are venerated, the saints' pennants hoisted, and special services are held in the churches. Bells toll ceaselessly, day after day, across the green valleys of the Creuse. The last *ostension* took place in 1988, the next in 1995 and so on, maintaining a tradition that goes back almost certainly to pagan times. As for those scraps of ribbon in the trees, 'fairy' trees are found all over western Europe, notably in the remote or Celtic districts, where two thousand years after the coming of Christ, the Old Religion still clings on.

From Lavaufranche the GR41, which overlaps the *Triangle des Combrailles* footpath hereabouts, took me south and east through country that was already beginning to undulate more and more, becoming distinctly hilly as the Auvergne grew ever nearer. By now I was searching for the mountains from the top of every hill, but the loom of the Massif Central was still out of sight. One certain indication that they were not too far away was the constant passage of jet fighters from the French Air Force. They were now flying very low indeed, never higher than the tops of the hills, and frequently below me in the valleys; always in twos, whistling up silently from behind to zoom overhead with a sudden startling roar from their engines. I saw and heard these jets almost constantly for the next two weeks.

After Lavaufranche the day settled down to the now familiar plod, forcing the miles away under my boots, through the green, spring countryside. This is a most agreeable part of France, quite untouched by tourism, full of little farms. The sides of the footpath were lined now with cowslips while, here and there, a water meadow running down to some unnamed stream would be carpeted with yellow daffodils. Somewhere along this path, I left my walking stick hanging on a stile and had to go back for it, for to lose my stick now would be a disaster. In any other country a stick is merely useful – to probe the depth of streams or bogs, as a third leg while fording rivers, or as a means of beating down nettles. These hazards are also encountered in France, but, as I said before, the real reason you have to take a stick is to fend off the dogs. Hardly a day, sometimes hardly an hour, went by without my having to brandish my stick at some aggressive, half-crazed dog, and although none ever pressed home its attack, I credit my unbitten progress mainly to my stick.

It is, I must add, no ordinary stick. Ordered by a friend, Paul Reynolds, as a good-luck gift, it was made for me by Theo Fossel of Beaconsfield, who is President of the British Stickmakers' Guild, and a real craftsman. As such, Mr Fossel was mildly put out when I took my stick back to have it shortened from shoulder height to a more convenient three-foot length. 'You're wrong, you know,' he told me. 'Once you get used to it, you'll find that length very comfortable, and since you will be crossing all sorts of country, very helpful. The rule is, the steeper the terrain the longer the stick. If you are going to exercise your dog in the park, something like a three-foot knob-stick will do – it scares the muggers off as well. I'll cut this down if you wish, but this stick of yours is really a classic, a shepherd's-length stick, in holly, with a carved horn handle. Stagecoach drivers used whips with holly shafts, you know, and carriage-drivers still do; it's a lovely wood. I use all the British woods for my sticks; hazel, ash, sweet chestnut or blackthorn. For the handles I use staghorn, which must be naturally curved because you can carve it but not bend it, or ram, ox or goathorn, which you can shape and carve and polish.' Theo Fossel sells hundreds of sticks every year, because after a lapse of generations, the stick is making a comeback.

'Before the First World War, everyone carried a stick – it was the mark of the gentleman or the country-lover. I think the Baby Austin killed the use of them – they couldn't find any room for it. But cars are bigger now and country pursuits are getting more popular. Most of my sticks sell for £10 or so, but you can pay as much as you like; it depends on the amount of carving. I sell a lot at between £10 and £50, and some go up to £300, but they would be beautifully carved, and carving like that can take up to four hundred hours – it's a craft. I'll make a few of those every year. I've even made bishops' croziers. A stick should be a good companion, but you'll find that out for yourself on your walk.'

That I did. So, weary as I was, I turned and retraced my steps to find the stick still hanging on the stile where I had left it an hour before.

With such diversions time passes quickly, and a very full day's walking brought me into the spa at Evaux-les-Bains in much better shape than I had been after walking a similar distance over easier terrain the day before. That's the way it goes though; it's all in the heart and the mind.

Evaux-les-Hains is a spa, the only thermal spa in the Limousin. As is the case with many spas, it is one which owes its existence to the Romans, who were much given to taking the waters and bathing in thermal springs. Evaux stands in a central position in

France, and that strategic location enabled it to survive even after the Roman Empire fell. It jogged on quietly until the last century when *thermalisme* became extremely popular in France. The present vast complex of baths and fountains was built around what is now the Grand Hôtel, in the years after the Franco-Prussian War of 1870, when the French spurned visits to Baden-Baden or Marienbad and sulked in the spas at home.

Personally, I am not a lover of thermal springs and take the usual smelly, luke-warm waters only with the greatest reluctance, 'in the interests of my readers', as the Ferrets would say. More interesting, from my point of view, was the fact that Evaux lies on yet another footpath, the GR460, *Le Sentier du Triangle des Combrailles,* a three-sided route, which I would follow round one side to my junction with the great GR4. Progress, progress . . . . I was going to make it to the Mediterranean after all – and meanwhile I had a hot, mineral spring to rest my tortured feet in.

Put simply, the Combrailles is a vast, forested plateau, although at least one French writer, Poirrat, has said that it is, like all the Limousin, 'a land of hermits, of knights and of fairies, a magic place'. One thinks of the Isle of Avalon, of the romances of the Round Table. More prosaically, a glance at the map reveals from the contour lines that the Combrailles, south of Evaux, and the gorges of the Cher, are undulating, well-watered lands of streams and small lakes, dotted with little farms and rushing rivers. Perhaps it is a magic place after all.

I began this long day, which would take me well into the Auvergne and the Puy-de-Dôme, with a walk down the D-road out of town, before cutting off east down into a deep river valley and up again to the heights above Château-sur-Cher, which marks the meeting place of three *départements,* Creuse, Allier and Puy-de-Dôme. The day was clear but chilly and since my route lay more or less directly south, I decided to abandon the GR41 which was settling in for some relentless hill-climbing, and follow the Pampeluze tributary upstream towards Vergheas. This made for pleasant walking through country that is not very different from my native Chilterns, with tall beech trees growing out of chalky soil, covering the ground with a carpet of rustling brown leaves. I crossed the River Cher just once, inching gingerly across the torrent on a bridge formed from a fallen tree trunk, then climbed a hill to rejoin the GR41-460 near St-Maurice-près-Pionsat and so into Vergheas, where the little church contains a Virgin that is said to perform miracles. The mineral springs certainly seemed to have worked wonders with my feet and I made good time over rolling country, under a blue sky decorated with scudding clouds, descending on the GR41 again at the Forêt de Drouille.

By now I was getting weary, but luck was with me because as I reached the great lake at Chancelade near Charensat, at about four in the afternoon, and began to walk slowly along the eastern shore, I came suddenly on the Hôtel de Chancelade, another little *logis,* set all on its own beside the lake, and though quite deserted, open for business. I decided to call it a day, fell in through the front door and became an instant celebrity.

'Ah!' said Madame Lanouzière, when she eventually emerged from the kitchen. 'You are surely the English walker? I will ring our local correspondent and tell him you have arrived.'

Although the surge of interest in my trans-France walk had quickly declined south of Caen, I was still meeting the occasional journalist, sent out by his paper to ambush the English walker, take his photo and return with a scoop. Being a journalist myself, I didn't mind this too much, because most journalists, whatever their nationality or paper, tend to be cheery, chatty souls, good for half an hour in a bar and, if they didn't mind the same answers, I had no objection to the same questions. Where was I going? How far did I walk per day? How many pairs of boots did I have? Was it not boring? Was I not lonely? And (at last!) what would I like to drink? One can see why alcoholism is the occupational disease of the scribbling classes.

Freelance writers, *pigistes* or *journalistes-independents* like myself, are not common in France, but in addition to their staff writers, many regional papers maintain correspondents or 'stringers' in the larger villages, each one charged with reporting on local events or affairs, and paid so much per line for anything they get in the paper. To such people, the arrival in their village of some mad Englishman crossing France on foot was a godsend, and a great change from the usual run of news about sheep dipping, the success of the football team or the old folks' annual outing to Clermont-Ferrand. The correspondent for *La Montagne*, however, had his own priorities and made these clear when Madame Lanouzière summoned me to speak to him on the telephone.

'I suppose I'll have to come and see you,' he said grudgingly, 'but I'm far too busy this evening, and I can't come tomorrow until I've finished milking my cows.'

That is not the sort of excuse you will commonly hear along Fleet Street, but that was the moment when I knew I had arrived in the Auvergne, for the Auvergnats are like that; they don't give a damn for anyone, God bless them. One of the many advantages of crossing France on foot or even on a bicycle is that you get a chance to meet the local people. When you travel by car, not only do you travel too fast, but you are also typecast or classified on sight, because the car is both a barrier to contact and a statement. Your licence plate says that you are foreign – or even worse, English – certainly in a hurry, probably a tourist, and because you have a car and can afford holidays, quite well off, and not likely to be interested in the important things of life, like the price of fertiliser, the amount of cheating at the *parc des boules,* or the virginity of the barmaid. Because the locals can learn all that about you at a glance, there is little need for them to know more. Besides, you will be gone in a matter of hours, so why bother?

With the walker, it's different. The walker comes in on foot, moving slowly; a hot, dusty, and often limping figure, flopping into the bar and needing a *demi*. Most people are friendly – given half the chance – and, given some excuse to break the ice, are often eager for a chat. Granted I speak French, which helps, but more than that, I like the French, which I think they can tell. I also have a *faiblesse pour les françaises,* but that's another story. I really can't understand that rancour against the French that lurks somewhere in the hearts of most Englishmen, but I think it must go back to the Hundred Years War, or even the Norman Conquest. Writing on the Battle of Agincourt, the historian Christopher Hibbert remarked that 'the English regarded the French with that mixture of reluctant admiration, envy and frustration that the five and a half centuries since have done little to change', and I think that sums it up. Put more plainly, the English think the French are awkward bastards, not because they are right but simply for the sake of being awkward. That may well be so in the political arena, but I have never met any reciprocal response or animosity while wandering on foot or by cycle through the French countryside. Mind you, my accent being noticeable, I am at swift pains to point out that I am English and not German. The French may let bygones be bygones, but the people in the small villages of rural France have long memories. The countryside of France is littered with memorials to the men of the Resistance, the *Maquis, fusillés par les allemands,* or those who died in some small, bitter fight or ambush during the last war. The wise visitor, particularly one travelling on foot, does well to watch his step.

France is not a homogenous country, whatever the tourist may suppose. It may be more centrally directed than Britain, with almost all the real power resting in Paris, but the local people possess and enjoy their differences. Plodding south, I met the Normans and Tourangeux, the Berrichois, and the Cévenols, all different, all French, but none to my mind is so different and yet so French as the Auvergnats of the Massif Central.

Just to begin with, they look French. North of the Loire, most of the local people are adequately prosperous and look much like anyone else; they won't thank me for saying so, but they could be British. Here in the heartland, it is different and no one could possibly mistake a typical Auvergnat for anything but a peasant from the central mountains of France. The typical Auvergnat is a small, squat, squarely built man, his heavy face suffused with a rich colour caused by good solid eating and plenty of drink. Most of the Auvergnats drink like fish. Just look at them as they crowd into the bar on any evening, and whatever the hour of day, there were always at least ten of them in any bar I entered. Even while I ate my breakfast croissant they would come into the bar for a bracing *coup de rouge* or a shot of Pernod, just to start the day off, a yellow cigarette permanently glued to the lower lip, their burly forms encased in those traditional blue overalls billowing out above stout, muddy boots, the cropped heads topped off by a slanting black beret, the nap glazed with age and grime, their little eyes darting round to take in the man in the corner, their grunting speech quite incomprehensible.

I have to declare an interest and say that I like the peasants of the Auvergne. I like their traditional independence, their don't-give-a-damn air, their love of the land. Once the ice has been broken, no people in France are more friendly to the passing stranger. Talk to one and within minutes you are part of their crowd, the drinks before you lining up on the zinc with startling rapidity, for the Auvergnats love any excuse for a party. The Hôtel de Chancelade lies almost in the middle of nowhere, but the bar that night was crowded, and in the next week or so I became a martyr to hangovers.

Three small Shetland ponies were cropping the grass in a small garden beside the road as I came down the steps of the Hôtel de

Chancelade next morning and set out again down the GR41. These little ponies, which the French seem to use rather as hairy lawnmowers, stopped grazing for a moment and watched me fade out of sight into the trees.

Sitting over breakfast in the bar at Chancelade, I had taken another look at my route. In view of the fact that the Puy de Sancy, 5,900 feet above Le Mont-Dore was snowbound and the GR4 footpath across it still effectively blocked, I would need to divert around this crest and find another way to Cantal and the south. Therefore, to maintain my schedule, I would need to save a little time up here and could do this only by veering off the GR41 at some point and cutting off a corner to shorten my walk by a day's stage of twenty miles or so. As always there was a snag, and the snag here was the River Sioule, which lay directly across my path. Dammed somewhere downstream for a hydro-electric barrage, the Sioule was now a long, wide lake with only a limited number of crossing points. I could, for example, cut east from Chancelade to the crossing at Pont du Bouchet. By crossing there, I would arrive at Les Ancizes-Comps with a clear run from there down the volcano country on the GR441, *Sentier des Volcans d'Auvergne* footpath from Montfermy – and I could hardly come all this way and not put my boots on that excellent footpath for a trek through the spectacular volcanic landscape of the Puy-de-Dôme. Still, I could achieve the same aim by continuing on the GR41 to Miremont, then either following the GR441 directly east or dropping south to get on to the GR4. This is a path I had to join sooner or later because it provided most of my route through the Auvergne. This seemed a good idea and for either path I must cross at Miremont, but after that the GR4 began a series of those irritating meanders, and lacking the GR4 *topo-guide*, which exhaustive searching in every shop I could find had still failed to produce, this might add to rather than subtract from the total distance I must cover. So, curses, did my present

Geoff Cowan and the author arrive at Beaumont-sur-Sarthe

Reaching the Roche Tuilière, near the Monts Dore

The *château-fort* at Alleuze

The fortified gateway of Marvejols

A green 'sotch' on the rugged Causse de Sauveterre

Up the green hill to the Ville-Haute of St Flour

The southern Causses Méjean

St Enimie on the Tarn

Waterfall by Muron

A crater lake, Besse-en-Chandesse

Camargue horses

The tower of the walled town of Aigues-Mortes

path, the GR41. I wanted to go south, and both were putting in a sweep to the east. Decisions, decisions . . . .

I used to spend most of the day like this. People often wonder what the long-distance walker thinks about while plodding his or her solitary way across the country. Feet, food and sex are said to be the major features running through the mind, but I find that much of my time – certainly on this walk – was taken up with constant calculations on time, routes and distances that must be covered over the next few days, and with constantly revising my schedules. For all my efforts and good intentions, I found that I could average only a steady three miles per hour, but if I could keep this up hour after hour, in seven hours – or eight allowing for breaks – I could get the bulk of the day's distance done. The calculations arose because not all this time was spent travelling in a straight line. Time would be lost groping for the way in close country, when the map had to be consulted all the time, or in searching for bridges over rivers and swift streams, in descending the zig-zag paths down steep hillsides, or in climbing over or crawling under a series of rusty barbed-wire fences, snagging my trousers and thinking gloomily of tetanus. My notebook is full of columns of figures and little sums, none of which reduced the distance by a single metre, but all of which kept me occupied – a kind of mental chess. It kept my mind from the throbbing inside my boots. Leafing through my notebook, I can also see that after Boussac the weather improved. Those pages where the ink has run become infrequent from then on.

So, stumbling through the woods south of Chancelade, I debated which way to go. When the moment of decision arrived which, at a present guess, would be after I crossed the Sioulet at Miremont, should I go east, on the GR41 to St-Jacques-d'Ambur? If I did I could go up to the Chartreuse de Port Ste Marie, which might be worth seeing, and then wander on to Montfermy where the GR4 (Aubusson to St Flour) came in from the west. Or should I abandon these GR trails altogether and cut south from where I now was to Gelles, then head directly west to the Puy-de-Dôme? From there I could carry on due south to Orcival, which I had on my list as a place I must not miss. How could I have my cake and eat it?

Somewhere near Les Dejets, an hour after leaving Chancelade, I noticed that the GR4 ran across the map a little to the south-west of the GR41. If I marched south on a compass bearing from the next landmark at Laurière, I must surely cut across it at, say, La Jugie, from where, as far as I could see – and here I cursed, yet again, that missing *topo-guide* and this small-scale 1:100,000 map – the path crossed the Sioulet, so there must be a bridge at Pellefort on the river. I need not go to Miremont after all. I set 180 degrees on the compass and ploughed south, coming out, in due time, by the brickworks at La Jugie. I found the GR4 waymarks, which I followed from there down a steep hillside to cross the river, leaving Pontaumur a little to the west. Using the compass again to head across country, I crossed the main road linking Pontaumur with Pontgibaud near Les Monts. This was a bit of the real thing. After all, following a well-trodden, waymarked GR is not essentially different from cruising down a motorway; all the decisions are made for you. Cutting across the lie of the land with map and compass, from point to point is, on the other hand, a very enjoyable art – at least until you get lost. Once away from the Sioule, I climbed steeply uphill onto a rolling, fairly open plateau, and there I was rewarded with my first view of the high peak of the Puy de Dôme, far away to the west.

I had made it. This was definitely the Auvergne, the best walking country of France. From then on, whatever the difficulties, I never thought I would fail to make it to the Med. South of that distinctive hill, tipped with snow and crowned with a radio mast, a long line of extinct volcanoes marched south to the barrier of the Monts Dore. These are the volcanoes which formed the Auvergne, and they are the distinctive physical feature of this part of the Massif Central. Some have craters, some do not. Some of the craters contain lakes, while others have been almost blasted apart by eruptions or the lava flow. There are over a hundred extinct volcanoes in the *Chaine des Dômes,* in a line which runs south from the Sioule to the Puy de Sancy, and very spectacular they look too, especially on those rare occasions – like this particular day – when the mist or heat haze lifts and their green cones stand out sharply against the far blue sky.

Walkers like different things, different kinds of terrain . . . some like the woods and the gentler green country, others are never really content unless the scree is slipping from under their boots and rattling away down some vertiginous crevasse. My taste lies somewhere in the middle. I like ridge walking, views, vast misty vistas and a sense of space. I find the high mountains claustrophobic.

The Auvergne is the ridge walker's paradise, especially here in the volcano country of the Puy-de-Dôme, where eruption and erosion have scraped the hills bare, softened the cones, and smoothed the hillsides into gentle contours. As you climb, the countryside expands, rather as if it were taking in one deep breath, and when you arrive, panting, at any one of a hundred crests, the countryside ripples away on every side, green, misty, entrancing; mountains you just ache to put your boots on.

These mountains came more clearly into sight with every kilometre I walked down the minor road to Gelles, my head tilted to the left, the sun blazing on my face. I found, as so often, that I should have put some water in my water-bottle and, when I stopped to get some at a farmhouse by Les Betz, the farmer offered me some wine to go with it, clomping up the stairs in his wooden clogs to fetch the bottle. He had never met an Englishman before, he told me, although sometimes their cars came past and they waved at him out of the window. Were the English friendly? They were, I told him. Ah, but did they like the French? Most of them do, I said, but he seemed a little doubtful. I found that sort of attitude frequently in the country districts of

France, for received opinion is hard to argue away. Deep down, the English secretly believe that the French wear striped jerseys, eat snails, play accordions, carry strings of onions about, are far too interested in sex, and have not enjoyed the civilising benefits of cricket. In return the French feel that the English inhabit a gloomy, fog-shrouded island, eat boiled cabbage, wear bowler hats, worship *le fair-play*, and are often homosexual. Meeting an English walker, who chats in French, drinks their wine, and seems (for an Englishman) normal, is therefore something of a shock. He came out to wave me off and was still there in the doorway, staring after me, when I looked back from further down the road. I faded out of his sight like a mirage on that shimmering, hot day, and half an hour later, were it not for the empty glasses on the kitchen table, he might have doubted my very existence. I followed the road round the conical hill by Tracros, and came out on the ridge high above Gelles, just as the evening sun gathered itself up and swept down across the western sky. Three hundred miles now lay behind me, and ten days crossing the glorious and green Auvergne lay ahead.

CHAPTER SIX

ACROSS THE VOLCANO COUNTRY

'Tell me a story,
That nobody knows,
And show me a country,
Where nobody goes.'
Anon

The mountains of the Massif Central are immensely old, far older than the Alps and the Pyrenees. This may account for the fact that these Auvergne peaks are much lower than those found in those other, more famous ranges; the highest point hereabouts, the Puy de Sancy, at 6,174 feet lies far below Mont Blanc, which towers up to 15,766 feet and is the highest mountain in western Europe. But the Auvergne is, as the name itself implies, a land of summits. Time may have eroded them away, smoothing out the higher peaks and the sharper edges, replacing sheer rock walls with soft, green rounded hills – the tops of which offer vast views – but if so, this suits me very well, for I am no great lover of the high mountains. I like the open ridge country, full of space and sky. For someone who enjoys such things, the Auvergne offers the most perfect walking and the most striking scenery in France, a landscape dominated in the north of the Auvergne by the Monts Dômes – the sharp peaks or *puys* of long extinct volcanoes – then by the high and definitely mountainous barrier of the Monts Dore, and finally, fifty miles further south, by the Monts du Cantal. All of these ranges were formed by the action of ancient volcanoes. Well, perhaps not so

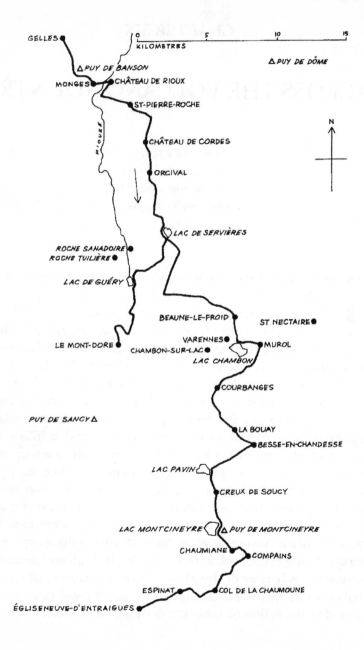

GELLES

△ PUY DE BANSON

△ PUY DE DÔME

MONGES

CHÂTEAU DE RIOUX

ST-PIERRE-ROCHE

M'OUZE

CHÂTEAU DE CORDES

ORCIVAL

LAC DE SERVIÈRES

ROCHE SANADOIRE
ROCHE TUILIÈRE

LAC DE GUÉRY

BEAUNE-LE-FROID

ST NECTAIRE

VARENNES

MUROL

LE MONT-DORE

CHAMBON-SUR-LAC

LAC CHAMBON

COURBANGES

PUY DE SANCY △

LA BOUAY

BESSE-EN-CHANDESSE

LAC PAVIN

CREUX DE SOUCY

LAC MONTCINEYRE

△ PUY DE MONTCINEYRE

CHAUMIANE

COMPAINS

ESPINAT

COL DE LA CHAUMOUNE

ÉGLISENEUVE-D'ENTRAIGUES

0   5   10   15
KILOMETRES

N

118

ancient in geological terms, about two million years, and who is really to say if they are not dead but sleeping? Two million years is barely a nap for a volcano.

I swung into the Auvergne from the west, entering the northern *département* of the Puy-de-Dôme with great glee and stopping for the first night at Gelles, with the green-peaked volcanoes of the Puy-de-Dôme now clearly in view. There are more than eighty volcanic cones running south across the Puy-de-Dôme for more than twenty miles, creating a countryside that is marvellous to look upon. Gelles lies in a wide valley and on the previous evening I had been glad simply to get there, lurching painfully down the hill in the still, warm, evening sunlight, to collapse into the bar of my hotel on the main street, calling loudly for a *demi-pression*, and swearing that tomorrow I would, this time I really would, fill up my water-bottle. Water weighs, but without it the walker on a hot day can quickly become seriously dehydrated. I drank a considerable amount of water that evening before I began to feel well again, and I went to bed early, quite exhausted. As usual next morning I felt much better and, with no great distance left to go before Orcival – at least by the standards I had set over the previous week – I took an hour or two off to wander round the town.

Gelles is a small, square-cut little place at the foot of some low, jumbled hills, a typical Auvergnat town, with silver walls and black-tiled roofs, overtopped by the church which is in the Romanesque style. It stood, that morning, with its doors wide open, as is the fashion hereabouts. Among the memorials inside the church is one which gives thanks to Our Lady of Orcival for saving the town from burning and the inhabitants from massacre during the summer of 1944, when the German Army and, in particular, the 2nd (Das Reich) Division of the Waffen-SS came rampaging through the Auvergne.

When the Allies swept ashore on those beaches west of Ouistreham in June 1944, many German divisions, especially their all-important armoured divisions, were resting and re-equipping south of the Loire, beyond the immediate reach of Allied airpower. Once the Battle of Normandy began, with fierce fighting on the plain around Caen, these armoured divisions were needed urgently and set out for the north, but as soon as they moved, they came under attack from the French Resistance, the *Maquis*.

Even today, feelings in France are mixed about the *Maquis*, not least among the old *Maquisards*. The popular view is that the Resistance saved the honour of France during the Occupation, and this balances out the fact that France collaborated with the Nazis in many areas of policy, not least in the deportation of the Jews. Not all the *Maquis* were keen to engage the enemy; some, the *refactaires*, fled to the hills to escape forced labour in Germany and, while some of the Communist groups were very active, others preferred to husband their strength with the aim of staging a military coup in France in the immediate aftermath of the war. I can recall meeting one old *Maquisard*, who told me sourly that he saw far more 'Resistance men' at the post-war celebrations than he ever saw in the field during the war, but as Britain, apart from the Channel Islands, was never occupied, this is an area where even Francophiles can offer little helpful comment. By mid-1944, the *Maquis* had risen to a fighting strength which exceeded one hundred thousand men and women, well-trained, adequately equipped by air-supply, and organised in local groups. Some of these groups were largely composed of *refactaires*. Some were aggressive groups led, or trained, by French or British officers parachuted in from Britain, while others were made up of local people – farmers, office workers, housewives and doctors who went about their affairs during the day and took up arms at night, sallying out to ambush convoys, blow up railway lines, kill motor-cycle despatch riders, and generally make the lives of the occupying forces a living hell. Sometimes, as on the Vercors plateau or at Mont Mouchet to the east of the Auvergne, the *Maquis* would assemble a considerable force and challenge the German Army to battle in the field, but for the most part it was a small, secret, vicious war between the local people and their foes, and the outcome of these local conflicts is still plain to see.

France is littered with memorials to these fighters, to countless thousands of nameless, hopeless fights, or to vicious, murderous reprisals. As they marched north in the post-invasion months of 1944, the German divisions turned on their tormentors or roused the local garrisons against the local people. Hostages were taken, prisoners shot, whole villages deported. Hardly a village is without its martyrs, and many places saw some appalling sights, as at Tulle, where the 2nd SS brought their *Maquis* prisoners into the town and hanged them from lamp-posts along the main street, only stopping when they ran out of rope, or at the village of Oradour-sur-Glane, near Bellac in the Limousin, which the 2nd SS surrounded on the afternoon of 10 June 1944. They rounded up the entire population and paraded them in the main square, men, women and children; then the killing began. The men were taken to one side and machine-gunned. The women and children were driven into the church, the door was locked, and the church set on fire with flame-throwers. Then the whole village was put to the torch. The Germans killed 642 people in Oradour-sur-Glane, over two hundred of them children. They shot the village priest and the doctor and the school-master. They shot old Marthe who was over seventy, and little Mayre who was only six. They shot her sister too.

I did not attempt to discover what went on in Gelles when the 2nd SS passed through; some things are not improved by detail. I left the church and went back to the hotel for my rucksack, and by nine was trudging out of town, heading for a day off in Orcival.

Gelles is no great distance from Orcival, at least as the crow flies, and I marched there on local footpaths, or by following a compass bearing. I was now in the no-man's land between the GR4 and the GR33, and decided to pick my way to the GR33, first up and round the wooded top of the Puy de Banson, which was a chilly spot early in the morning, with a keen wind whistling through the trees. A little south of here I picked up the GR33 and followed this east through the village of Monges, down a steep hillside and across the railway line to the ruined castle of Rioux, thinking that I could reach the GR41 – the *Tours des Volcans* - and so be in easy reach of the intact and inhabited castle of Cordes, only a few miles south of Orcival. Then I got lost.

I missed the waymarks, set the compass for a direct route towards the turrets of Cordes, which I thought I could detect directly ahead, glinting in the glare of the eastern sun, and found myself descending a very steep hillside into the River Miouze. This was not my intention, but that is the problem with using small-scale maps. Cursing, I made my way back up the hill, found the main road and crossed it on to a minor road into St-Pierre-Roche, a very pretty spot, and descended to another wide, rushing river. Here a large Charolais bull came snorting over to the far bank and stopped for a closer look, which made crossing here a little risky. I turned to walk upstream, the bull following me along the far bank until stopped by a fence.

The path then veered away from the river and began to lead me west, so I cut off and climbed up the hillside through thick beech woods; and then I stopped to think. If I kept heading east on the compass bearing, I must reach the GR4-41 and could turn south along it for Orcival, but first I had to descend the hillside and cross this river, a rushing torrent which I could hear somewhere far below. Scrambling down the hillside proved difficult, for it soon became quite sheer and I descended, ape-like, crashing through the bushes, swinging from branch to branch of the close-set beech trees. The slope fell directly into the stream without a bank or a path, so I continued to play Tarzan among the trees above the river, while I sought a way across. When I finally found a bridge it was only a slender tree-trunk set just above the torrent, with a strand of barbed-wire strung across it at thigh-height. However, in moments like that, any bridge will do. I tightened the waist-belt on the rucksack and began to inch across.

I was halfway across the river, edging nervously along the trunk, when it became very clear that I was about to fall in passport, money, cameras and all. Deciding to accept the inevitable, I tightened the rucksack again, held the cameras over my head, and jumped. The rushing water came up to my chest. Actually it was quite pleasant and very soothing to my hot feet. I splashed ashore to the far bank, well upstream of the bull, and was practically dry by the time I had found the GR4-41 waymarks on the far hillside, and followed them to the driveway of the château of Cordes.

Cordes is well worth visiting, for it is a truly beautiful little place, a dream-like, fortified manor built in the late fifteenth century at the time when gunpowder was rendering medieval castles obsolete. The gardens and parterres are full of box-hedges and ponds attributed to Le Nôtre, and they set off the small, neat turrets of the castle to perfection. My particular interest in Cordes lies in the fact that it contains the tomb of Yves d'Allegre, who was the companion in arms of Cesare Borgia during the Pope's attempts to unify Italy, and who was killed at the Battle of Ravenna in 1512. Yves liked Cesare Borgia, and says as much in his memoirs. 'I have heard all that men now say about the Duke,' he wrote, 'but for my part, I remember only that he was a good and generous companion and a valiant man-at-arms.' Machiavelli took an equally approving if more pragmatic view: 'Upon a thorough review of the Duke's actions and conduct I see nothing worthy of reprehension in them. For as he had a great spirit and vast designs, he could not well have acted otherwise than he did in the circumstances.' Cesare came to a sticky end, fighting in Spain, and his bones now rest under the doorstep of the church at Viana in Navarre, where all men can step on them, but Yves has come to a more fitting memorial. His tomb in the chapel at Cordes is quite magnificent, a suitable resting place for a great soldier, but then the Auvergne has been producing soldiers and patriots since ancient times, as Julius Caesar discovered when he marched this way in 54 BC.

The Arvernes, the Gallic tribe who lived hereabouts, led the resistance against Rome, under the leadership of their war-chief Vercingetorix, and forced Caesar to raise the siege on their *oppidum*, or hillfort, at Gergovie. This lies a few miles north of what is now Clermont-Ferrand. Caesar counter-attacked and was driven off with losses, but that was the high-water-mark of Gallic resistance. In the following year Vercingetorix was defeated, surrendered at Alesia in Burgundy, and was taken to Rome, where he was led in chains behind Caesar's chariot, and strangled. *Vae victis*, indeed.

From Cordes the GR41 footpath climbs up the castle drive to the main road. It then veers off east for views towards the snowcapped heights of the Puy de Sancy further south, before descending into the valley of the Sioulet to Orcival. The small town is dominated by and famous for its twelfth-century pilgrim church, which contains the shrine of one of the Auvergne's most popular saints, Notre-Dame d'Orcival. The local guidebook notes that the shrine is the object of veneration and frequent pilgrimages. The Virgin of Orcival, 'Our Lady of Irons and Fetters', is also the patroness of captives and on the south wall above the main door hang an assortment of manacles, even a ball and chain, brought there by prisoners after her intercession had obtained their release. The church of Orcival, built of dark volcanic rock in the Romanesque style, dates from the twelfth century and is said to be the most beautiful church in the Auvergne. It is certainly very striking. The Virgin of Orcival is only one of several Virgins remembered by the Auvergnats, who are much given to the cult of Our Lady. There are others at Clermont, Vassivière, Auzon and Ambert. Some of these are 'Black' Virgins, but the Virgin of Orcival sits on her throne in the usual Auvergnat style, and is not black at all but covered with votive silver and bright enamels.

Orcival is a pleasant spot, and a tourist centre for the *Parc des Volcans d'Auvergne.* This regional park was created in 1977, and is the most extensive of parks, covering the Auvergne ranges from the Monts des Dômes in the north to the hills of Cantal, three days' march to the south. Orcival itself is quite small and sheltered in the Sioule valley from the chill winds sweeping in from the Puy de Dôme or the Puy de Sancy, full of pleasant hotels, and a good centre for touring the Puy-de-Dôme *département,* but in mid-April it was almost empty of tourists. I dumped my pack and wet boots in the Hôtel de Roch and then, since this was early in the season and the dining room was closed, I went off to eat at the Hôtel Notre-Dame just across the street, where Josette Daldini and her son Nicolas were all smiles. 'Nicolas wants you to sign his autograph book,' said Josette. 'He thinks you're the most famous person who has even been here.' This was very gratifying if rather doubtful, but Nicolas is a nice lad, busy helping his mother with her work, so I duly signed, even promising to send him a postcard from the Mediterranean when I eventually arrived there – a promise I remembered and kept.

Meanwhile, Josette was charging about the room, serving a dozen people at once, uncorking wine, delivering plates, passing menus and getting the cheeseboard circulating. Why anyone thinks that running a country hotel would be a restful occupation for their retirement beats me. Over the coffee, Josette, whose husband is in the *Armée de l'Air,* described a day's routine which begins at 6.30 a.m. and usually lasts until after 11 p.m., with steady toil all the time and outbreaks of increased activity during lunch and dinner. 'Yes, it's hard work,' she said, 'but it's a living and around here, apart from tourism, there is no other work, so . . .' she shrugged, 'I do it. And in the winter it is quieter – and I enjoy it. Did you enjoy your dinner?' I did.

Not even the fiercely proud Auvergnat would claim that his Auvergne is one of the great gastronomic regions of France, on a par with Normandy or Périgord, but the local people are interested in food, and that is half the battle. Riding my bike to Compostela one year, I recall stopping at the Hôtel Sarda, near Monistrol d'Allier in the Margeride, which is run by an Anglo-French couple, David and Joelle West. 'The Auvergnats love their food,' Joelle told me. 'Quite often we get groups coming in with Fr3,000 or more to spend and asking, "What can you do us for that?" Well, for Fr3,000 we can do quite a lot. Most of the spare cash hereabouts goes on food.' I can't say I had many memorable gastronomic experiences in the Auvergne, but I ate very well and needed to, just to keep going.

Unemployment and depopulation are the twin scourges of the Massif Central, the reasons why this otherwise delightful part of France is being steadily denuded of people and why tourism, with all its risks and corrupting influences, is seen as a lifeline for the local communities. This was brought home to me next morning when pretty Christine Pacaud came over from the *Comité de Tourisme* in Clermont-Ferrand to bring me a comprehensive and very heavy press-pack, full of leaflets, and tell me a little of the local history, and the causes of the present decline.

'We have to go back a bit, to the end of the last century, when the Paris-Nîmes railway came through here. At first that made life more interesting and easier, because we could then send our three main products to Paris.'

'Three products?'

'The Auvergne had carbon – charcoal – from the forests; cheeses – Cantal, St Nectaire, Bleu d'Auvergne – and wine. But then the phylloxera killed the vines, and the market for charcoal collapsed. Cattle, milk and cheese are not enough to live on, so the people had to go away to work – and they still do. Some of our communities have lost fifty per cent of their population in the last ten years, and more people are now dying than being born here. It's so sad. People go away to work and if enough go away there are no passengers for the bus, so it stops, and not enough children for the school, so it closes, and then people who might have work here still have to leave because their children must be educated. Tourism is important to us because it not only gives money, it brings work that needs hands – waiters, maids, guides.

As it is, there are now more Auvergnats in Paris than there are in the Auvergne.'

Indeed there are; so many, in fact, that they have their own newspaper, *L'Auvergnat de Paris*, which makes fascinating reading. A love of their native land is one of the true Auvergnat's most endearing characteristics, and however long they have been in Paris they like to keep in touch with their home village and know, down to the smallest detail, what is going on there. *L'Auvergnat de Paris* therefore carries pages crammed with snippets of news from small villages all over the Massif Central.

At Miers, in Haute Loire, you will be sad to hear that '*Monsieur le Cure, fatigué, était absent pour Pâques*'. From Darnets comes the good news that at last *'Le chemin le long du cimetière est terminé'* . More good news too from Malfont, where Denis Bourdon has got his driving licence, and from Lorlanges where Monsieur Riffe went fishing and '*a pêché six truites*'. In Mazerat, Roger Sauret has installed a metal garage and in Laval all the people who had colds feel better.

This need to keep in touch with their homeland seems deep-rooted, for the Auvergnats of Paris return often to their villages, so that cars with '75' series number plates, the number of Paris, are almost as numerous hereabouts as those with local plates.

Next morning I spent a restful couple of hours ambling around the sunny corners of Orcival, sending some postcards back to Britain, exulting in the distance covered so far, with no real problems apart from the perpetual agony of the footsore, and the rather startling discovery that, after about 300 miles, the cleated rubber soles of my boots had worn alarmingly thin. A careful trawl through two of the local bookshops failed to produce a copy of the GR4 *topo-guide,* but I did find one of the large-scale 1:25,000 maps, covering the barrier of the Monts Dore, just to the south, the next physical obstacle I must cross on my journey to the southern sea.

Having already saved a day by cutting off the GR41 and turning through Gelles, I decided to use part of my day off and gain a little of the distance on my next day's route across the Puy de Sancy. Leaving my rucksack at Orcival I walked up to Le Mont-Dore for a look at the mountains and a chat about conditions with the *Gendarmerie de Montagne.* This proved a very pleasant half-day walk, *sans sac-à-dos,* across glorious country first up the GR4-41 to the Lac de Servières which, from its circular shape clearly occupied the crater of a volcano, then over the hill, past the deep valley between the glittering schist-covered slopes of the distinctive Roche Tuilière and the Roche Sanadoire – both eroded relics of a volcano – and on across the *col* to the Lac de Guéry, blue and sparkling against the snowcapped hills. I finally arrived at Le Mont-Dore, just in time for tea.

Le Mont-Dore is a thermal spa in summer and a ski resort in winter. Today it is very much a tourist mecca, but it has roots going back to Roman times and is notable among British Francophiles as the birthplace of the popular Dordogne, which rises here as a rushing stream by the side of the public gardens. I had arrived in the week before Easter, in the 'tween-season lull, at a moment when, in spite of late snow flurries, the ski season was really over and the summer not yet begun. According to the *gendarmerie* I could go up the road towards the summit, but the ski lifts were shut and on the crest the snow was still deep enough to impede my progress across the summit. The Puy de Sancy is about 6,000 feet high and although I did not need the waymarks, which were under the snow anyway, and could head due south on a compass bearing to arrive somewhere on the far side, I was not too keen on the idea of forcing a passage over the crest. Walking in soft snow at such an altitude is extremely hard work, and the weather was still very changeable. I returned to Orcival by bus that evening and began to consider other possibilities, starting with a long brood over the maps.

From Orcival I could take the GR441 again as far as the Puy de l'Aiguiller, south of Lac de Servières, and then take a forest footpath across the top of the Puy Baladou on to a forest trail which ran south-east to Beaune-le-Froid, and so eventually reach Lac Chambon to the north-east of the Puy de Sancy. From there I could walk to Murol, which was said to have a mighty castle, and so to Besse-en-Chandesse on the GR30. This was longer than the GR4 route and out of my way, while Besse too was a ski resort and might well be snow-bound, but the contours on the map looked more reasonable than the direct path over the cloud-topped, snow-covered Puy de Sancy. Besides, I wanted to see the village of Besse-en-Chandesse, so this is the route I adopted and a very beautiful route it is.

Next morning I began again, scrounging a lift up to the point where I had veered off for Le Mont-Dore on the previous afternoon, cutting off the road and through the woods to the lake. From the Lac de Servières, the footpath climbed very steeply up a tussocky hillside, giving me an exhausting start to the day, but one which delivered me above the snowline well before midday. From here, high on the hill, I had good views all over Puy-de-Dôme, from the Monts Dore at my back, all up the line of volcanoes, past the Puy de Dôme itself, that distinctive peak topped with a radio mast, on the blue Monts Dômes in the misty north. Seen from here, the Monts Dômes are quite remarkable, soft circles of old volcanic cones set like green whorls in the landscape, with the Puy de Dôme itself rearing up to 4,806 feet, right in the centre, and the focus of all eyes for miles around. The ground on which I now sat was dark volcanic earth, littered with large, weathered, green or red lumps of lava, spewed out in some eruption countless millenia ago. Behind me, a little south, lay the long line of the Monts Dore, with the Puy de Sancy, the highest peak in France outside the Alps and Pyrenees, now in plain sight, but with no movement visible on the snow-slopes facing north. This is beautiful, breathtaking country, perfect for walking, magnificent to look upon, and I had at least another week of it before I reached the limits of Cantal – a delightfid prospect.

This was the Thursday before Easter, and with spring now well advanced, I was a little surprised to find plenty of snow about on the tops and langlauf skiers sliding and gliding on my path. They were not all that pleased to find my footprints on their *loipe*, but fortunately I did not have to stay on this snowbound trail for long and could soon cut east, descend a ridge and pick up the forest trail that led me east to Beaune-le-Froid, which has a beautiful Romanesque church and a very welcome bar, both of which were open. The '*le-Froid*' suffix comes from the fact that there are ice-caves in the hills just above the village, where ice used to be stored for use during the summer months, in the days before refrigerators. The bar-keeper's lady put me on the right footpath and, following this south, I soon found myself on the hill above Varennes, descending steeply to the lake at Chambon on a beautiful spring day.

Chambon-sur-Lac, which has yet another of those splendid Auvergne Romanesque churches – one of some 250 churches in the Puy-de-Dôme which are entirely or partly Romanesque – lies just west of the lake which, like Servières, occupies a volcanic crater. This lake was created by the *Volcan du Tartaret*, which exploded and formed the lake as recently as ten thousand years ago. To the north of the lake stands a tall cliff called the *Saut de la Pucelle,* the Maiden's Leap, from which a young shepherdess hurled herself, hoping to escape the clutches of a lecherous knight, and landed unhurt at the bottom. This feat went completely to the girl's head and she boasted of her miracle so often that the local villagers suggested she leap off a second time, which she did . . . splat! And so to Murol, drawn on by the sight of the massive castle on the hill above.

I had lunch in Murol, then took a taxi up the hill to inspect the mighty castle, which is open to visitors and the centre for continuous *spectacles* with some of the local people – *Les Compagnons du Gabriel* – in medieval costume, acting as guards or knights or wenches.

The castle at Murol dates from the thirteenth century and the great encircling wall was added only two hundred years later. The castle somehow survived intact until after the Revolution, when it was gradually dismantled as a source of dressed stone, until it was granted the protection of the Beaux Arts. Rightly so, for Murol really is the most splendid pile. The Auvergne is a land of castles, so many and so fine that there is a *Route des Châteaux d'Auvergne,* which leads the visitor around a selected thirty-nine of the finest. Most of these are my favourite style, medieval *châteaux- forts,* and while some – like Tournoël near Volvic – are in ruins, others – like La Roche at Aigulperse, the Château-Dauphin near Pontigibaud, Châteaugay, Cordes, mighty Busseol near Vic-le-Conte, the classic lakeside Château de Val near Bort-les-Orgues, Anjony and Auzers { are all intact and quite perfect.

Three miles to the west of Murol lies the little village of St Nectaire, where the cheese comes from, but I had to miss it as time was pressing. Half an hour at the castle was enough, even for mighty Murol; then it was back to the village to collect my pack from the restaurant and off south again along the GR30. That afternoon was a truly beautiful walk, through open rolling country on a sunny day, first up a wide track to Courbanges, and then down to the farm at La Bouay above Besse. This is a high plateau, all sheep and stream country, and I spent a lot of time crawling under or climbing over fences, losing the cocking handle off one camera somewhere on the way, having to wade across shallow streams from time to time. Every stream contained a fisherman spinning for trout, and the tinkle of water was everywhere. I lost the GR30 some way past the Puy des Prêtres, where it swung off towards Super-Besse, but this mattered not at all as I now had old Besse in plain sight.

Besse-St-Anastaise is a medieval town, and one which has retained much of its encircling walls and towers, notably the Porte du Ville, which still has a protected sixteenth-century outwork designed to protect the main gate from cannon fire, and the Tour de la Prison, which was once the town gaol. Old Besse is a pleasant town to stroll about in, with a maze of narrow streets to explore – especially the Rue de la Boucherie, lined with old buildings built in that dark volcanic stone – sheltering here from the hot afternoon sun, or lurking in the Church of St Andrew, which is built mostly in my favourite Romanesque and contains a famous Black Virgin, at least in the winter months. On 2 July each year, the Black Virgin of Besse is carried by the men of the village to her chapel at the Lac de Vassivière, and stays there until the autumn. The Virgin of Besse is a formidable lady and it is said that when, in 1547, one of the local merchants passed her chapel at Vassivière without lowering his head, she struck him blind, restoring his sight only when he repented. This miracle so impressed the local people that they transferred her statue to Besse, but next day it had vanished and after a search was discovered back at Vassivière. This happened three times before the locals understood her message and repaired the chapel where she now spends three months of the year. When she returns to Besse on the last Sunday in September, the bells are rung and the whole town celebrates with dancing and fireworks during the *Fête de la Montée*.

Sitting before a beer on the warm terrace of the Hostellerie du Beffroy, I decided that diversions from my main axis of advance which led to places like Besse ought to be encouraged. Even so, my next task must be to get back on the GR4 and head south. I began this task next morning with a very early start and a stiff climb to the snowline at Lac Pavin, near the ski resort of Super-Besse, four and a half miles west of the old town.

Lac Pavin is one of the beauty spots of the southern Puy-de-Dôme. It is a beautiful place – a deep, blue, circular crater-lake set among dark green pines – and on this cold spring morning the water was still covered with a thin skin of ice. The GR30 footpath circles the lake for a while, gradually climbing the crater walls before coming out briefly into open country and heading south through the woods where it joins the GR41. Here, sheltered from the sun, the snow still lay ankle-to-knee-deep on the path, under breakable crust. The snow faded away as I came out past the Creux de Soucy into glorious open country, the one part of the entire walk that now, months afterwards, remains most strongly in my memory. It was Easter Monday, a public holiday, and yet the countryside was empty. I walked slowly south across the soft, springy grass, over meadows sewn with daffodils and threaded with tinkling silver streams towards my first landmark, the dark, forested cone of the Puy de Montcineyre. This loomed ahead, but of the lake at Montcineyre I could see no sign, which worried me because, according to my map, it lay just to the west of the path and was a large lake, quite impossible to miss. So was I lost?

I came down a slope almost to the foot of the hill, crossed a rushing stream on stepping-stones, passed a *gîte*, and then the lake came suddenly into view, wide and blue, completely surrounded by steep green slopes dotted with patches of snow, with the Puy de Sancy rearing up against the blue sky beyond. It was quite breathtaking. Places like the shores of the Lac de Montcineyre are enhanced by an absence of people, times when there is only the quiet crunch of your boots along the pebbled shore to break the silence, and only an eagle circling in the sky to add movement to the scene. I was, and still am, entranced by this country of the southern Puy-de-Dôme, and pleased that you can really only get into it on foot. I shall go back to the Lac de Montcineyre, but it will never be quite the same as it was on that still, bright morning in spring – second visits never are.

South of Lac Montcineyre the GR41 climbs up to Chaumiane, where a small farm was surrounded by fields deep in daffodils, then drops steeply down to the pretty village of Compains, which has several hotels and a restaurant, all of which were open. Why I ever worried about finding food or accommodation during my walk across France remains a mystery. The only result was the burden of a rucksack full of camping gear I had had no reason to use, so I made the mental resolve to unload some of the weight at the first opportunity. I could tell it was too heavy because every Frenchman I met would pick it up and, raising his eyes, say 'Ooh-la-la!' I dumped it on the ground at every stop, or rested it on fences or walls, but the weight still crushed me over the course of a long day. I had a rest and lunch sitting in the sun on a terrace at Compains and, having made good time so far that day, was in no great hurry to leave, but I was still east of my real path, the GR4. At Compains I left the GR41 which went off towards Brion and, since the roads were quiet, I took the D26 up to the Col de la Chaumoune, a stiff climb which led to the top and a small, cool *buvette* just in time for a beer. Then due east on the D30, an even more minor road across country past a couple of small lakes, before turning into the hamlet of Espinat. Here my arrival was greeted with the usual cacophony from a pack of dogs, which streamed out of the barns and houses and had to be driven off with flourishes of my stick, and help from a local farmer.

A footpath ran on from Espinat to my next night-stop back on the GR4 at Egliseneuve-d'Entraigues, and I strolled south along it in the warm afternoon sun, lopping the heads off the dandelion clocks with sabre-like sweeps of my walking stick, until I was roused from my day-dreams by a great deal of bellowing and an alarming sight on the path ahead, where a large herd of cows was making a rumpus.

I am not afraid of cows. I am sensibly wary of bulls, but I was brought up on a farm and know that the majority of cows are placid creatures, much given to mooing, chewing the cud and lying down when it looks like rain. Most cows know their place, but those spilling now across the path ahead were not like that at all. I have ridden on a cattle drive across Montana and these Auvergne cattle would not have looked out of place on the Wild Western prairie. To begin with, they had horns. Not longhorns perhaps, but certainly horns-and-a-half – each one offering a spread from tip to tip of three feet or more – and sharp, black-tipped horns at that. Even worse, these horns were clearly meant for use. Several of the cattle were sparring together fiercely, their horns rattling, making a sound like a stick drawn hurriedly along a fence. Others were using their horns to plough up the soil, then kicking the dirt and dust up over their backs with sharp backward thrusts from their hooves. All this took place to the sound of moos which were more like bellows or trumpeting than the usual placid farmyard noise. I stood, hesitating, on the path as, one by one, the cows saw me and turned to stare. Cows are curious creatures, and as they began to trot towards me, I dodged off the track and took to my heels, running for the shelter of the barns.

Days later, I read in one of the *topo-guides* that these brown, horned, Auvergne cattle were 'often curious, rarely fierce, but still best avoided'. I liked that 'rarely'. Rarely indicates 'sometimes' and when you are on foot in open country, even once could be enough. I played hide-and-seek with these snorting monsters all around the farm buildings for half an hour or more before I was able to break away and run up the far hillside, slithering under a fence as the first hairy brute came thundering up after me. Panting, I hurried off across country to cross the GR30 once more – what a wandering footpath it is – and followed it down the hill to Egliseneuve-d'Entraigues at the end of a wonderful, exciting day in the southern Puy-de-Dôme. There was only a short distance left before I could put another *département* behind me by crossing the border into the county of Cantal. The weather seemed to have set fair, I felt fit, and the glorious walking of the last few days, across the hills from Gelles, had given me the taste for more. All Cantal and the Gévaudan still lay ahead – terrific. I crossed the river, keeping to the shady side of the street, and was in my hotel, boots off and glass in hand, by just after five in the afternoon.

CHAPTER SEVEN

CROSSING CANTAL

'Spring seduces,
Summer thrills,
Autumn saddens,
Winter kills.'
Keeners Dictionary

At Egliseneuve-d'Entraigues I was still – though only just – in the Puy-de-Dôme, but on the threshold of the next, most southerly *département* of the Auvergne, Cantal. From the hillside above Egliseneuve I could look down on the roofs of this little town, which stays tucked out of sight in the valley of the rushing Rhue until almost the last moment, and by lifting my eyes a little, I could look south to the still-distant peaks of the Plomb du Cantal, the relic of yet another volcano. Those peaks, I noted, were also covered with snow. Egliseneuve-d'Entraigues is just a dot on the map, but it turned out to be quite a substantial place on the ground, with several hotels and restaurants, all of them open for business on this Easter Monday afternoon. It was for places like this that I had lugged a full set of camping equipment half way across France, only to find, once again, that I need not have bothered.

My initial thirty-plus pounds rose a little almost every day, partly because, squirrel-like, I gathered up brochures and leaflets from every hotel and lunch-stop on my way, but mainly because every tourist office and *Syndicat d'Initiative* presented me with a press-pack of information on the local attractions. With this book

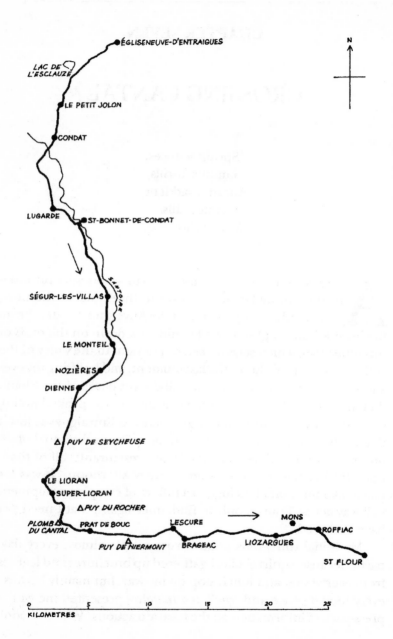

ÉGLISENEUVE-D'ENTRAIGUES
LAC DE L'ESCLAUZE
LE PETIT JOLON
CONDAT
LUGARDE ● ● ST-BONNET-DE-CONDAT
SANTOIRE
SÉGUR-LES-VILLAS
LE MONTEIL
NOZIÈRES
DIENNE
△ PUY DE SEYCHEUSE
LE LIORAN
SUPER-LIORAN
△ PUY DU ROCHER
PLOMB DU CANTAL ● PRAT DE BOUC   LESCURE   MONS   ROFFIAC
△ PUY DE NIERMONT   BRAGEAC   LIOZARGUES
ST FLOUR

0   5   10   15   20   25
KILOMETRES

138

as the final objective, I was very reluctant to reject information I might need later at home. I ditched leaflets on *thermalisme* or the making of cheese, while watersports on the local reservoirs did not seem too compelling, but all the rest I kept – and it got heavy. I had another brochure clearout after I had washed my socks that evening, celebrating the Easter holiday by treating my now travel-stained Rohan jacket to a long-overdue scrub in the shower. I hung it from the window in the warm evening sun and it was dry again inside an hour, so I put it on and went out to explore the town. This didn't take long.

Egliseneuve-d'Entraigues is a resort town, a centre for summer walkers and, since the two often go together, cross-country ski-tourers, who flock here in winter to ski in the wild, open country that lies to the west of the Rhue, towards the Plateau de l'Artens. That apart, the main attraction in Egliseneuve-d'Entraigues is the *Maison des Fromages,* where an exhibition, audio-visual and tastings, will tell visitors more about the four cheeses of the *Appellation d'Origine Controlée d'Auvergne* (Cantal, Bleu d'Auvergne, St Nectaire and Fourme d'Ambert) than they really want to know. Thank God, the *Maison des Fromages* was closed, but to explain that relief I must go back a bit. The only time I have ever felt truly sorry for a member of the Royal Family was when I read that Prince Charles had been taken on a full-day visit to a ball-bearing factory in India. This sympathy dates back to the time when my guide failed to turn up on a ski trip, and the hosts decided to fill in the time by taking me to a cheese factory. There, *noblesse oblige,* I overplayed my hand. 'Really?!' 'How interesting!' 'As much as that . . . ?' 'Goodness . . . !' This feigned interest proved my undoing. Over lunch, with the guide still missing, my hosts said that as I had been so interested on the morning visit they had fixed up another one for the afternoon.

It is fairly easy to get lost on the way out of Egliseneuve, because there are a great number of *ski de fond* trail markers about. Two great footpaths, the GR4 and the GR30, also coincide here, and I had no *topo-guide* to either. However, my usual evening reconnaissance of the route and some advice from the barman in the café across the road from my hotel put me in the right direction. Next morning, I followed the GR30 east up a steep hill and along a track which soon turned into a stream, splashing along until a signpost pointed me up a grassy bank onto the GR4. Here the footpath runs across that open, short-grass ridge country that I personally prefer, and which – with the occasional forest and deep ravine – I would cross on much of my journey south and east from this point, at least as far as St Flour.

A little south of Egliseneuve, just past the Lac de l'Esclauze, I entered Cantal, famous for its cheese and for the mountains which now lay ahead, the Monts du Cantal. I had to cross these somewhere above the ski resort of Lioran. They were still two days' march away, and showing up now as a thin line of snow-capped peaks. Meanwhile I had this beautiful, rugged country to cross on the way down to Condat. More of those wild Auvergne cattle lay in ambush beside the path, gathered together on top of a small rocky hill and descending with a great clattering of hooves to line the far side of the electric fence, moo-ing aggressively as I strolled past, flourishing my stick. The GR4 ran on, past the farm at Le Petit Jolon, which stood in a sea of daffodils, and then plunged down a steep hillside to Condat, which lies deep in the valley and, like Egliseneuve, remained out of sight until I was practically on top of it. The sun was now well up and very hot, so this seemed as good a place as any to stop for my midday *demi-pression*.

Condat occupies a valley where three small rivers converge and is pretty enough, but apart from a cold beer, the village had little else to detain me and the gorge of one of the rivers, the Santoire, soon provided the route out. The Santoire runs just to the east of the GR4 footpath, so I followed it south, along the cliff-edge to Lugarde, before dropping down into the gorge and walking in to St-Bonnet-de-Condat. I was driven off the hill because, having yet again forgotten to fill my water-bottle back in Condat, I was already very thirsty. There was neither shade nor water up on the open hillside, and I soon became dehydrated.

Thirst may seem an out-of-place problem to develop in the middle of France, but the water supply can be strangely erratic deep in the wild, even here in the green Auvergne, where one is rarely far from a spring or a river. I have been thirsty many times on my travels and I know all the signs that tell you to get hold of some water before you succumb to heat exhaustion; the dryness in the back of the throat, the fact that your tongue seems to be too big for your mouth, talking to yourself. At least on foot I have never yet plunged to that depth of exhaustion I have met on cycle-tours; that sudden energy collapse that cyclists call 'the bonk', which comes on very quickly and takes hours to go away. But heat is my enemy, and I prefer to wait out the hot midday hours until the sun abates at around four o'clock. I came plodding down off the hill, drank deeply from the tinkling feed-pipe of a cattle trough and walked slowly on into pretty St-Bonnet, quite ready for a rest in the shade.

Like any village of any size hereabouts, St-Bonnet had a couple of small, pleasant hotels, where I could have stayed, but even after a rest it was still only three in the afternoon, which seemed far too early to stop, even if the sun was blazing down and I was already very tired. I decided to follow the road for a while, passing under the shadow of the railway viaduct which spans the valley below the Chapel of Our Lady of Valentine, which stands high on the eastern hill. After brooding on the possibility of a diversion towards Allanche, I stopped for the night in an excellent little *logis,* the Hotel Santoire, which claims to be in Ségur-les-Villas but actually lies two and a half miles further south at La Carrière du Monteil. On the way there I rested up in another of those dark, cool little roadside *buvettes*, which was run by the usual old lady in black, and arrived at the Hotel Santoire just in time to claim the last room and meet the owner, Monsieur Chabrier, who is not only a keen walker, but was going to London the following week. My low rat-like cunning surfacing yet again, I thundered back upstairs to load superfluous kit into a stuff-sack – all the press-kits, the broken camera, my tent, the mattress, redundant socks, a torch – and shot back downstairs to the bar before the welcoming *bonhomie* could fade. Monsieur Chabrier willingly agreed to transport my surplus equipment back to England and leave it with a friendly tour operator. He also suggested a good route across the hills to Lioran, so it was with a light heart and much lighter rucksack to heave on to my back that I set off next morning across the plateau du Limon for Nozières and Dienne and the long climb from there up to the snowline and down the far side of the Alagnon gorges to Lioran.

My departure from the Hotel Santoire was hurried along by a small posse of dogs from a nearby farm, which came hurtling across the grass to snarl at my heels. As I reached the hill above Le Monteil, the early-morning sun, which had anyway seemed far too bright, tucked itself away behind the black rain-fringed storm clouds. The fine hot days of the weekend had gone and there was work-a-day weather all the way into Dienne, but I was snug inside my windproofs against the sweeping drifts of rain and hail, and got the first half of the day's walk completed long before noon.

Dienne is another pretty village of Cantal. Its very fine Romanesque church contains a thirteenth-century carved statue of Christ and is topped off with a most impressive open belfry. As I emerged from my visit to the church, three monks in grey habits entered, and seconds later the church bells began to toll. That doleful sound followed me right across the valley, up a footpath and through the woods onto the snowline above the Lioran valley, where the sun came out, and I got gloriously lost. This was the first hint of a problem that was to plague me over the next week as I went higher, I went back into winter. Crossing Cantal, it was not at all difficult to meet three seasons in a single day, simply through alterations in altitude. In the valley, the sheltering walls cut the wind and encouraged the spring flowers to spread their petals, but as I climbed, I reached a level where the trees were still unbudded, while on the tops, at 4,000 feet or more, there was still snow and often a chill, shrieking wind. All in all, it kept me on my toes.

If there were any waymarks here on the tops they were well covered by snow, so I simply took a bearing on the Plomb du Cantal, the highest mountain hereabouts, and followed it south as best I could. Lioran, I knew, lay at the foot of that looming peak. This move was not entirely wise, for I came out somewhere below the summit of the Puy de Seycheuse, to find myself near a group of barns, old *burons*, with no visible way down the far side. After hours scrambling down rock ledges, edging across a sheer cliff halfway down a waterfall, and then crossing a mountain stream in full flood, I finally picked up a local footpath and staggered out on to the main road under the Roche du Bec de l'Aigle, half a mile or so east of Lioran, at four in the afternoon, dripping with sweat and quite exhausted by the heat. Fortunately, no stream or standpipe had been left untapped along the way, so I soon had my breath back and was able to turn up the hill, plodding slowly into Lioran and my night-stop at the Auberge du Tunnel. After an hour there resting on the bed in my dark, shuttered room, I felt up to a little more walking and decided to go out and explore. Besides, I desperately needed the local 1:25,000 map, for my walk on the morrow must be a long one across deserted country. I also wanted to find the point where the GR4 led out of Super-Lioran, which lies on the hill above the hotel, up to the summit of the Plomb du Cantal, at 6,180 feet the second-highest peak in the Auvergne.

The Monts du Cantal are topped off by two *puys*, both the relics of one gigantic volcano. The Puy Mary, to the northwest of Lioran, and the Plomb itself which rises up behind Lioran, are popular skiing areas, their slopes well supplied with lifts and a cable car which runs from Super-Lioran up to the summit of the Plomb. The Plomb bars the main road and rail link from St Flour to Aurillac, and although there is a road across in summer, the passage is facilitated by two long road and rail tunnels bored through the mountain in the middle of the nineteenth century. The Auberge du Tunnel, standing at the eastern end, was once a coaching inn, a place which still retains that slightly gracious nineteenth-century air, with low beams, copper pans and sparkling glass on the table.

Exiting from the Auberge du Tunnel is quite hard work, out the back door and up a long series of steps to the upper level, but once up there it is only a mile or so uphill to Super-Lioran, the new, or new-ish ski resort that now occupies the upper slopes of the Plomb and the slopes of the Monts du Cantal between the Plomb and the Puy Mary. On this afternoon, Super-Lioran was rather a sorry sight, as most ski resorts are once the winter snow has gone. The shop-keepers were removing their stock and closing down for the summer, the lifts hung silent, while crowds of French day-trippers mooched about the centre, wondering what to do. The weather was mixed, warm enough when the sun was out, suddenly chill when a large black cloud came slipping past its face. A shredded mist and low cloud blew about the Plomb, sometimes descending as much as halfway from the summit. The GR4 fingerpost, set right in the centre of what in winter was the beginners' ski slope, pointed impassively east, up the steep sides of the mountain into that grey mass of cloud.

Quite suddenly, matters began to look more serious. I returned to a café, ordered a beer and sat down to brood over tomorrow.

Having come to Lioran, I must climb the Plomb du Cantal if I was to follow the GR4 to St Flour. Anyway, the Plomb fascinated me for another reason. Years before I had made a ski tour, in terrible weather, across the more southerly Aubrac plateau. Every time the blizzard abated, our guide would lead us up to the nearest crest, point north and announce, 'From here, on a good day, you can see the Plomb du Cantal'. Yet because we never actually had a good day on that otherwise enjoyable trip, the Plomb remained an unseen attraction until I came over the northern slope of the valley on this walk. Even then it was a fleeting glance with cloud, rain and snow flurries sweeping over the top. Nevertheless, for some reason it seemed important to climb across the Plomb. If I didn't, then in some way I would have failed.

The Plomb du Cantal is a high mountain and the country beyond as far as St Flour, the *Planèze*, is both wild and empty, and I had just disposed of a tent and my full range of hard-hitting gear, all of which was now London-bound in the boot of Monsieur Chabrier's car. If anything went wrong on the next day, I might be in serious trouble, but in my experience life is like that. Years ago, while serving in the Royal Marines Commandos where I learned much of my low rat-like cunning – I had noticed that when we went out on one of our periodic bashes, everyone took far too much food and, once the weight began to tell, started to dispose of it. It was therefore quite possible to live well on the mountain while carrying a much reduced weight uphill, simply by gleaning rations from the tins dumped by my sweating comrades up ahead. All would have been well if I had had the sense to keep this useful discovery to myself. Unfortunately, I mentioned it to my cronies, and they mentioned it to their cronies, and the word got around. On our next expedition into the wild, we all left our tins behind and travelled hopefully but light. Four days in the Scottish Highlands with nothing to eat but boiled sweets is not a pleasant experience and my reputation suffered.

So, typically, I had discarded my hard-hitting gear just at the point where I might need it! I walked slowly back into Super-Lioran and consulted the gallant lads of the *Gendarmerie de Montagne*, the local mountain rescue team, who were somewhat non-committal about my prospects.

Did I have rain gear, a good map and a compass? Well, I would also need a map of minimum 1:25,000 scale – my 1:100,000 scale was much too small and really no good at all. This I knew. As for the *météo*, the forecast was very mixed, with rain, low cloud, mist, sun, all possible. The best idea was to go up to the summit in the morning and have a look. If it looked tricky, and especially if the visibility was poor, I would be well-advised to come down again. On the other hand, if I was now in *pleine forme* and could use a compass, I could hardly go wrong – unless I twisted an ankle miles from anywhere. Their tone implied that I could do what I wanted but not to come crying to them if I got into trouble.

Whatever some may feel, I find this *laissez-faire* attitude rather refreshing. Many British hill-walkers, or at least those British hill-walkers who write to me, seem to be safety-mad. Given that some thirty or so walkers perish in the British hills every year, there is some justification for their caution, and no one is more cautious I. If I think the conditions are that dangerous, I don't go out at all, but if the letters I get are anything to go by, many of my correspondents are so cautious that I can't see how they ever get past their own front doors. I have little doubt that this passage will produce droning letters written in green ink on lined, recycled paper, accusing me of feckless frivolity, and luring ramblers from the leafy lanes of Surrey to a miserable death in the remote hills of the Auvergne. My attitude clearly meets with some strong disapproval, but what can one do about that? I'm just recounting my own experiences. I thanked the *gendarmes for* their advice, and found a shop which sold me a 1:25,000 map that covered most of the ground between Lioran and St Flour. Then I ambled back downhill to the Auberge du Tunnel, all set for a good dinner, a good night's sleep, and an early start in the morning.

Dinner was an enjoyable meal because Monsieur Lebas, the owner and chef, took me under his wing, inviting me to leave my lonely table and join him and his staff at their meal in the bar. Monsieur Lebas was a large, jolly man, so heavily swathed in his floor-length chef's whites that he seemed to run about on castors. Dinner was taken sitting on stools at a long, low table set beneath the television set so that everyone could watch the late evening film. Watching the film, passing dishes and chatting to Monsieur Lebas kept me so busy that it was some time before I noticed that the chair on my left was occupied by the hotel's large, fat, Alsatian dog, which was contentedly wolfing a bowl of pasta. This was a little startling but not as unpleasant as the sight I saw a few days later – a lady sharing a bowl of strawberries and cream with her poodle – first a spoonful for him (lick), then a spoonful for her ... disgusting.

A great gust of rain blew in the window as soon as I opened the shutters next morning. This was more or less what I had expected, because the weather is usually the opposite of what you want. On balance, though, I would rather start the day with rain, which may pass over by mid-morning, than begin with that bright sunshine which rarely seems to last out the forenoon. I packed quickly, dragged my rucksack down to the foyer and had breakfast, foraying out from time to time to see what was happening to the weather. By the time I was on my second cup of coffee the rain had stopped and it seemed possible to proceed, so I said goodbye to my hosts, climbed heavily up the flight of steps that led from the hotel to the upper terrace and walked up the hill to Super-Lioran, which was quite deserted at a little after eight o'clock in the morning.

The GR4 is well waymarked out of Super-Lioran, but the path itself lay up the line of a drag lift running between the trees, and was therefore under snow. The path was steep, icy, and very hard work, but I pressed on slowly, up onto a chill, windy upper slope and then, after an hour or so, on to the *col* between the Plomb du Cantal and the Puy du Rocher. Parts of this climb were nerve-racking because if I walked on the firm ice the effort was less but the risk of a slip from my now smooth boot-soles and a long fall thereafter was quite high, while if I walked in the snow, I went in up to my knees and soon became exhausted. In practice I compromised, choosing the ice when the risk of a long slide seemed small, enduring the soft snow when the path was more exposed. Once on the *col* a brief moment of sunshine gave me my first clear look at the long-awaited Plomb du Cantal. The cable-car which I might have taken up to the summit for a reconnaissance but had not been in operation when I passed it far below, suddenly sprang into life and droned upwards on my right, and a snow-flattening Rat-trac ground its way past, forcing me into the rock wall. But as I plodded over the top of the *col*, the eastern slope opened up below. From there I could see that not only were several of the drag lifts operating on a hillside still deep in snow, but that the slopes between me and the dimly-seen buildings of Prat de Bouc far below were alive with skiers. It had taken me some two hours to pant my way up from Lioran to the summit, and in the hope that the summit café might be open, I picked my way across the *col* to the top of the Plomb du Cantal.

The café, inevitably, was shut. From up here, it said in my guidebook, there is 'an immense panorama' which reveals all the *puys* of Cantal, the outline of the Margeride far to the east, and with luck, the Rouergue – the modern Aveyron – far to the south. At that moment, which was about ten in the morning, I could see for, well . . . yards. Any GR4 waymarks were under the snow, so I took a bearing on the Prat through a brief break in the cloud and then set off downhill, plunging forward instantly in a

148

knee-wrenching fall into a pile of ice-crusted snow, rolling down the slope to the bottom, shedding a camera, my hat and stick along the way. Plunging about in soft snow and collecting all my missing items quite wore me out, and my sudden arrival on the piste had not pleased the skiers, several of whom came slithering up to shoo me off the run. On the piste the snow was firm enough to walk on and I sank in only to the ankles, but the open slopes were soft crust and the snow often concealed streams. Inside half a mile I had twice plunged in waist-deep which, apart from a soaking, gave me a good fright.

Getting down to Prat de Bouc, which has a warm and very welcome café, took well over an hour, and I was soaked to the skin long before I arrived, forced on by the rain and low cloud that came sweeping in from beyond the Puy Mary, bringing hail to rattle hard on the shoulders of my windproofs. Once inside the old converted *buron*, the girl behind the counter took my anorak off to the kitchen and I dried myself a little by sitting on a radiator and playing with the café dog, which was an expert at catching lumps of sugar. This was one of the few friendly dogs I met during my walk across France. I lurked in this *buron* for half an hour, until the worst of that particular rainstorm had passed over, then climbed into my full range of storm wear and set off again, none too happy. Most of the morning had gone and, though damp, chilled and a trifle fed up, I still had more than twenty miles to do before reaching my next night-stop at St Flour and, if I could do it, my next day off. From Prat de Bouc the GR4 runs across moorland, a desolate place, dotted with abandoned and ruined *burons*, abandoned because no one wants to stay up in the hills these days and press the cheeses of Cantal, as they did in days gone by. This great plateau, east of the Plomb, is the *Planèze*, created aeons ago by the lava-flow from the volcanoes, smoothed and eroded into open, rolling pasture, pretty enough on a warm summer's day, but very exposed at this time of year.

It was a frightful day to be alone out on the open moor, and the GR4 waymarks first became sparse and then petered out completely, leaving me to rely on the compass, for I had already walked off the 1:25,000 scale map that had got me across the Plomb du Cantal to Prat de Bouc. Using the small-scale 1:100,000 map, I skirted the cross by the Puy de Niermont, picked up the GR4 again near the village of Le Ché, lost it again before Lescure, found it again and followed it through Lescure, which was empty of people. I had walked south to Brageac before realising that the local *randonneurs* had been re-marking the route. The new way marks were not shown on my small 1:100,000 map, and were leading me in the wrong direction. Cursing, I decided to save a few miles by heading east with the compass, sticking to the places shown on my map, which brought me into Liozargues by the early evening, and here I stopped for a few words with a man trimming a hedge beside the path.

'How far is it to St Flour?' I asked, putting into words the one thought that had been occupying my mind for the last few hours.

Still snipping away, he pondered this question for a moment. 'About nine kilometres,' he replied at last, nodding his head and pointing down the path, '*Tout droit*... you can't miss it.'

For their own peace of mind, I must advise all walkers in France never to ask such a question. It is also advisable, especially at the end of the day, to avoid taking note of the distances on French roadsigns. I walked on down the footpath for another half an hour, and came out into the main road near Mons, where a fingerpost right said 'St Flour 8km'. A kilometre stone, just in sight further down the road said, when I reached it, 'St Flour 9km'. This I found interesting. I was walking towards St Flour and it was moving away from me. I plodded downhill on blazing feet to Roffiac, and although Roffiac was at least two miles from the road junction I had passed half an hour or more before, the signpost there said 'St Flour 8km'. I felt like weeping. Even worse, they had built a bypass round Roffiac, and all the roadsigns promptly disappeared. I sat in a café, resting my throbbing feet, and gave myself up to hating French *fonctionnaires and* feeling sorry for myself, though in any other mood, Roffiac would have been appealing. It has an attractive Romanesque church and the pencil-slim tower of an old *château-fort* beside the river, as well as several hotels. Perhaps I should have stopped there, but there is that bloody-minded streak in me somewhere, so I heaved on the rucksack again and plodded on through the sprawling suburbs of St Flour in search of my hotel. As an old Compostela pilgrim, the only hotel for me in St Flour was the Hôtel St Jacques, but where the hell was it? I knew it lay in the *Ville-Basse* and as St Flour is a hill-top town, I thought I must surely reach *the Ville-Basse* first, but it didn't work out like that. Inevitably I entered St Flour along a high ridge, and finally, deep in the *Ville-Haute*, I asked a youth in a bus-shelter for a short cut down the hill. As he was heavily engaged in pawing his girlfriend at the time, my enquiry was none too welcome and his reply unhelpful. There was no short cut, so I must follow the road, round and round (and round) the hill. I just managed to say thank you and, a lifetime later, finally reached level ground and crawled, whimpering, up to the bar of the Hôtel St Jacques.

At this point, I might admit that there is a certain dichotomy in all this, as the ever-blunt Estelle pointed out while typing the manuscript. ''You might explain exactly why you are doing all this. You keep saying the walk was supposed to be fun, but you drone on and on about your feet and the rain and the heat and the exhaustion. I can't help feeling you enjoy tormenting yourself and you know what people say about people like that, don't you?' Yes, I do, but I don't usually care what people say. As my old Scottish grannie used to remark sagely: 'You wouldn't worry what people thought about you if you realised how seldom they thought about you.' I find that comforting. Another of her timeless gems was: 'Blessed is he who expecteth little, for he shall not be disappointed.' Someone else, no wiser than my grannie if more famous, Samuel Butler, has said that 'Life is the art of drawing sufficient conclusions from insufficient premises', and since all these sayings appeal to me, they must have some relevance to my attitudes. Truthfully, I don't really know why I like to take off across the world, on foot or bike, accepting whatever happens after that as a matter of course. I can't honestly say that I enjoy it, and no one has less objection than I have to the soft life.

Neither is it a need for excitement. Being a writer can be many things, but it is never, never dull. Neither are my trips an extension of Estelle's thinly hinted self-flagellation; I can get enough of that at my desk, but that's all right because I like work. When I'm sitting here, as now, working, on Sunday afternoon, I'm happy, and if long hours and hard graft are the price I have to pay for the life I want to live, that's fine by me. So, getting back to the point, why walk across France if I have enough challenges here at home? The short answer is that it's exciting.

In Hannibal's Footsteps, Bernard Levin's account of his walk from Aigues-Mortes to Italy, he reflects that as we grow older the need for challenges grows stronger, and concludes that for a man to '. . . emulate the doings of his own youthful self is very satisfactory'. I think there is a lot of truth in that, but as a motivation for tackling physical challenges I am less certain. Since spending the formative years of my youth in the Royal Marines Commandos I have tried to avoid all physical challenges like the plague, but at the same time I admit that they do have a certain fascination, providing one competes only with oneself.

Anyway, whatever masochistic urges, if any, lurk in my psyche, there is considerable satisfaction in setting oneself a task and then completing it. The satisfaction is increased when that completion becomes difficult. Indeed, unless it is (a bit) difficult, I don't see the point in attempting it at all. When people asked me what it was like riding my bike across Turkey, Syria and Jordan, they probably expected either a paean on the beauty of the scenery or a harrowing account of the snags. Both of these I could have managed, but thinking about it, all I could come up with, was 'Character-forming'. That trip reminded me, as this walk did, that you can do almost anything you want to, if you will but put your mind to it. Difficulties are simply opportunities seen in a different light.

Sitting here at home, on a summer Sunday, feet up and a cup of tea at my elbow, that seems to sum it up, but back there in St Flour it hardly seemed so obvious. Still, after an hour's rest and a long soak in the bath, I managed to make it down to dinner, though walkers in similar circumstances may be glad to know that the Hôtel St Jacques has a lift.

St Flour is one of the great cities of the Auvergne, and a very fine town it is, especially on a clear, warm day, when the weary walker can lie in bed late, drinking a pot of hot coffee while looking out of his bedroom window up the green hill to the *Ville-Haute, and* hugging the thought that on this day at least, he can take it easy, wear training shoes and walk no further than the nearest restaurant. I got up late, staggered about the room and into a hot bath, fingered over another coffee and croissant and, while I was at it, yet another Armagnac in the bar, before setting out to explore the town. This led to the discovery that there is, in fact, a short cut between the two halves of the city, up the steep, windy *Chemin des Chèvres,* the old goat track, which leads from the river, through one of the great gateways, and directly into the cathedral square.

*The Ville-Haute – or Vieille Ville –*is the larger part of St Flour, standing on the brink of a long ridge overlooking the 'new' town below, in the valley of the Lander. The *Vieille Ville* is a maze of narrow streets, lined with sixteenth- or seventeenth-century houses, for although the site is much older, much of the town was ruined during the Wars of Religion which ravaged France during the latter half of the sixteenth century. The cathedral is a dark fortress of a church, built in that now familiar volcanic stone, and dates from about 1400. With the hill to help it up, it is said to be the highest cathedral in France and stands at about 2,500 feet. The interior is one vast hall, containing some good glass and much fine wood-carving in the choir stalls, although the pride of St Flour is the great black crucified Christ, called *Le Beau Dieu Noir,* which hangs beside the High Altar. This being Easter-time, the *Beau Dieu Noir* was draped with the red robe of martyrdom. The cathedral also contains the relics of St Flour, who evangelised the Auvergne in the fourth century. The town became the seat of a bishopric in 1317, and survived the ravages of the Hundred Years War rather well, although as 'the key of France, the lock on the frontier of Guyenne', it was frequently besieged by the English. The locals say that only the force of the wind has ever overwhelmed St Flour, and windy it is, with a very chill northern gust scouring the streets that morning, forcing me to café-hop in an attempt to stay warm.

Bookshops are among my favourite places and I was seduced into spending a contented hour before lunch searching for more of those useful 1:25,000 maps – and no one has searched for buried treasure with more assiduity – while getting to know a little more about Cantal by leafing through some of the local history books. One of these was a fairly gruesome publication, a handbook prepared in the seventeenth century by the town executioner, which listed, among other details, his complete scale of charges. A whipping cost ten *livres,* a branding fifteen, cutting off a hand at the wrist twenty-five, a burning at the stake forty plus the cost of the wood – thirty *livres*-worth of wood was deemed sufficient to burn a normal-sized person. I hid this masterpiece away at the back of the shelf and hurried off for lunch. Fortunately, the Rendezvous des Pêcheurs, Monsieur Albisson's excellent restaurant, was open.

The food of the Auvergne, though usually of the simple rib-sticking variety, can be exceptionally good, and no praise is too high for the freshness and quality of the local produce. I ate very well in St Flour, during dinner at the Hôtel St Jacques and here at the little Rendezvous des Pecheurs by the river, which serves local dishes *de l'Auvergne pures et pas trop dures*. This is farmhouse fare, perfect for the weary walker; *aligot* (a local speciality of mashed garlic, potatoes and cheese), a little *coq au vin*, a slice of apple pie and a selection of cheese, the *bleu d'Auvergne*, a piece of *the fourme de Cantal*, from Ambert, and a bottle of local wine from St-Pourçain-sur-Sioule. I floated back to the Hôtel St Jacques and spent the rest of the afternoon drowsing peacefully on my bed for, truth to tell, I felt very tired.

Geoff's attrition factor had reached the limits of its power by now. At St Flour I had completed more than 400 miles of my journey, across all kinds of country, and could cover my required daily distance, if not with ease then at least by gritting my teeth, ignoring the aches and pains and pressing on until the required distance had been covered. Even so, I felt pretty tired most of the time, because when a man gets over fifty he doesn't bounce back as quickly after a gruelling day in the hills as a younger man might do. I found that the effort, and in particular the effort of will required to complete each stage, did not, in fact, diminish — some form of mental battle was going on most of the time, so I was very glad that I had Geoff's plan with me, a programme where every stage was set out as a daily target. I did not have to think about it, I simply had to do it, and if I succeeded, then I had the bonus of a good hotel every evening and, now and again, even a day off.

That evening in St Flour, I creaked my way downstairs for dinner, chatting first to Monsieur Prat over a *kir* at his bar, with Virus, the family poodle stretched out asleep on the counter beweeen us. The Hôtel St Jacques was built in the eighteenth century as a hostel for pilgrims heading south to join the great Santiago pilgrim road that runs across the Aubrac plateau from Le Puy to the valley of the Lot. Monsieur Prat took me into the dining room to point out the stone carving of a Santiago pilgrim on the mantelpiece above the fireplace. The fact that I had been to Santiago de Compostela myself, riding on my bicycle all the way across France and Spain, from Le Puy in the Vélay to the good city of the Apostle in a distant corner of Spain, seemed as good a reason as any to go back to the bar for another drink.

When I got back to my room later that evening, I opened the window and looked out along the edge of the river to the night sky, now glinting above the dark bulk of the *Vieille Ville*, while cold air rushed past into the heated room. The stars were like splinters of mirrored glass so, with luck, the weather tomorrow would be just right for walking: dry and sunny and not too hot. The last week had taken more out of me than I could afford to lose, and I still had a long way to go.

CHAPTER EIGHT

MARGERIDE, GEVAUDAN
AND AUBRAC

'If this is the best of all possible worlds, where are the others?'
Voltaire

The way out of St Flour lay across the Pont Neuf, which stands just by the Hôtel St Jacques, a *pont* that did not look very *neuf* to me. The next leg of my journey lay down two regional footpaths or *GR du Pays*, first the *Sentier du Haute-Auvergne*, and then the *Tour des Monts de l'Aubrac*. A *sentier du pays* falls somewhere between an unadopted local footpath and a national *sentier* of the *Grande Randonnée*. These routes have been chosen by the main regional walking group which, in the case of the Haute-Auvergne footpath is CHAMINA, the outdoor organisation which covers the Auvergne, and it is therefore waymarked with the *GR du Pays* slashes of red and yellow paint. These waymarks began on the old bridge, which gave me a good start, and the morning was bright and breezy, which was fortunate. When I returned through St Flour three weeks later, heading home, a blizzard was blowing and most of the countryside thereabouts lay deep under snow; and this in May! Auvergne weather tends to be changeable, and snow lies in St Flour for five months of the year, but my luck held – just – throughout the journey. So, feeling fit and rested after my day off, I swung along in fine style, at least to begin with.

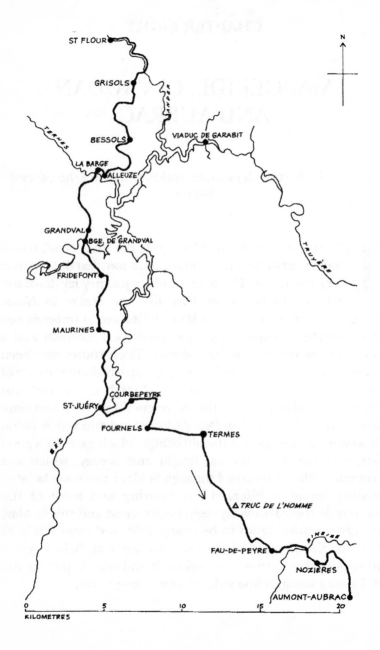

ST FLOUR

GRISOLS

BESSOLS

VIADUC DE GARABIT

LA BARGE

ALLEUZE

TERNES

TRUYÈRE

GRANDVAL

BGE. DE GRANDVAL

FRIDEFONT

MAURINES

COURBEPEYRE

ST-JUÉRY

FOURNELS

TERMES

BÈS

TRUC DE L'HOMME

FAU-DE-PEYRE

RINÈSE

NOZIÈRES

AUMONT-AUBRAC

0   5   10   15   20

KILOMETRES

'South!' remained my constant cry, but here as elsewhere, my direct route to the Mediterranean was barred, this time by the great reservoir at Grandval, which stores up the River Truyère as it flows from the Margeride, forming it into a vast lake with deep inlets spreading far up into the side valleys. It left me with a choice of just two crossing places: either over the road-bridge under Eiffel's great railway bridge at Garabit to the south-east, or on the road which runs across the Grandval dam itself. Both offered distinct attractions. The viaduct at Garabit is one of the wonders of the Industrial Age – a fantastical structure which soars high across the Truyère gorge, and carries the railway line which runs from Paris to Nîmes. Eiffel took two years to build the Garabit viaduct, between 1882 and 1884, and it was because of his success here that he was later commissioned to design and construct his famous tower for the Paris Exhibition of 1889. Heading south under, or even across, Eiffel's viaduct, would be an attractive addition to the route but it would take me out of my way. Grandval, on the other hand, lay near enough due south, actually on the *Sentier Haute-Auvergne,* and a long day's walk south on this footpath would take me to St-Juéry in Lozère, and so put another *département* behind me.

So, in the end, I chose to cross the Truyère at Grandval, not least because this meant I could keep to the Haute-Auvergne footpath. Any footpath is preferable to the straightest road. In addition this footpath leads south beside the gorges of the Ander to the beautiful fortress at Alleuze, on a route which, if I simply kept going, should deliver me to my night-stop at St-Juéry by the late afternoon.

The path out of St Flour first crosses a footbridge over a stream, then climbs around the side of the hill above the Ander, giving great views back across the *Ville-Basse* towards the fortress city on the hill. Halfway up there is just the place to stop and take some photographs of the upper town, before emerging, after less than two miles, onto a farm-dotted plateau. From there it was south through the villages of Grisols and Bessols to the woods overlooking the Ternes, where the *château-fort* of Alleuze stands on a spur overlooking the river.

Looking east from any high point along this route, I could see the dark forests of the Margeride, one of the most beautiful and deserted regions in central France. Like the Aubrac further south, the Margeride is part of a vast plateau – *La Plaine* - hurled up aeons ago by volcanic action. It occupies much of the country between the Truyère, which lay at my feet, and the River Allier further east, which marks the western edge of the Vélay. It is a wild, beautiful, desolate, empty land, melancholic even. Years ago, heading west for Compostela, I had ridden across the southern part of the Margeride on my bicycle, and can still remember the total silence wrapped around me on those empty mountain roads.

Alleuze, on the other hand, is a very romantic spot. The square keep, with a tower at each corner, stands as a castle should stand, on the summit of a small hill, a place of golden stone set against emerald green forest, with blue water lapping gently at its foot. The GR footpath leads out to the edge of a vertiginous hill, high above the castle. It took the long zig-zag downhill path quite a while to deliver me, boots skidding on the stones, at the door of the chapel that lies just across the road from the castle, below the village of La Barge. I dumped my pack here, lapped water from the stream and then set out to explore. On such a brisk morning, a place like Alleuze is well worth crossing all France for – even on foot.

The fortress of Alleuze was built in the thirteenth century by the Constable of the Auvergne, the King's lieutenant for that troublesome region, but it soon came into the hands of the Bishops of Clermont. They used it to collect local tithes and as a prison. During the Hundred Years War it was held for the French, and then captured in 1383 by a celebrated Gascon free-company captain, Bernard de Garban, who used it as a base while he pillaged the surrounding countryside for his lord, the Plantagenet King. He finally consented to depart in 1391 after receiving an enormous bribe from the people of St Flour. The bishops moved their troops in once again, but since men-at-arms were expensive, the Bishop's garrison rarely exceeded five men. There they stayed until 1405, when the people of St Flour, fearing that the castle might again be captured and used as a base by the ro*utiers,* fell upon the castle one night and demolished the outworks, until all that remained of the castle is the single keep we see today.

The little Romanesque chapel at the foot of the opposite hill dates from the same period as the castle, and from there a line of white crosses marks a pilgrim trail to the calvary on the hill outside La Barge. As I had done enough climbing already, I left La Barge for another time, walking down the road and across the bridge over a tributary river, the Ternes. Then it was up and up, through the woods, over yet another hill to the escarpment that looks down on Grandval. Grandval village was deserted, a newish place built for the workers at the power station and, there being no one to ask, even an exhaustive search failed to produce any sign of a bar. I plodded slowly across the top of the dam wall. On the far side it was a climb through the woods yet again, with the top of every hill giving fine views east towards the great forests of the Margeride and past La Bastide. There, just beside the path, is a monument to ten men from the village of Fridefont, shot in June 1944.

Fridefont has an hotel, two bars and a church which contains a museum. I could not visit the museum because a service was in progress, which was a pity because this church contains the sixteenth-century Virgin of Mallet, wrapped in a green veil, which I had very much wanted to see. This day was the Day of the Deportation, a fête commemorating those men of France deported to Germany during the last war who never returned. I dumped my rucksack and returned to one of the bars for a beer, a chat with the owner, and a chance to sit in the shade.

'Do you know anything about that *Maquis* monument down the road at La Bastide? About the men named on it?'

The bar-lady, who had a small child on her knee, shook her head. 'They were of the Resistance – some of them. I know they were from this village. My parents knew them.'

'And do you know what happened? Was it an action? An ambush?'

'No. The Germans simply came one morning, took them away down the road and shot them.'

Beyond Fridefont the footpath runs along a ridge, giving a beautiful airy walk above the valley of the River Bès, another blue tributary of the Truyère. The gorges of the Bès are quite delightful and completely deserted, a fairy-like place of rocks, ferns and rushing water. I followed the river canyons from Maurines, which has another fine thirteenth-century church, all the way to the village of St-Juéry where, on the bridge, I crossed out of Cantal and into the *département* of Lozère, the former Gévaudan.

St-Juéry is a village that repays inspection. Surprisingly, for it is not all that small and is very interesting, it fails to rate a single mention in any of the Michelin Guides. I stayed only one night, but could happily have stayed a month and have every intention of returning there some day, but then I like small villages. I was brought up in one, and although in those pre-television days we had no entertainment at all except for fitful reception on a battery wireless, a church you went to twice on Sundays, one pub which you did not go to at all on Sundays, and one all-purpose shop, the days simply weren't long enough for all the things I found to do. The trouble today is that we rush about too much. Our so-called servants – the car, train, telephone, telex, aeroplanes and, above all, the television set – although supposed to make our lives easier and more entertaining, have actually become our masters. We dance to their tune, run ever faster to keep their schedules, and human beings though we are, run our lives to suit the pace of machines. There is something wrong there, and surely it does not have to be that way. All you have to do is live at walking pace.

Had I arrived in little St-Juéry by car, I would either have driven straight through or fidgeted to reach the road again, but my pace of life had changed in the last three weeks. I had slowed down, physically, emotionally, perhaps even mentally. Twenty miles now seemed a good day's journey, not just a ten-minute blast down the motorway. I was more than content to watch the hills come closer slowly, or take half an hour off to sit on a bridge, fascinated by the trout finning quietly in the water below. I was happy to while away the evening sitting over a beer with the old men of the village, people I had never met before and would never meet again, just chatting of this and that. It was a gentle, rather aimless kind of life which did no one any harm, and reached its peak with me in St-Juéry. It is worth reiterating that not once on my walk did I feel a foreigner. Somewhere in the Bible, and I wish I could find it, there is an instruction which says, as I remember, 'Be thee ever mindful to entertain strangers, for many, so doing, meet angels unawares'. I doubt if the ever shrewd French mistook me for an angel, but their hospitality to this particular stranger must surely earn them a place where angels are not uncommon, if they only get their due.

On the way in to St-Juéry I had been worried that I would find no more comfortable accommodation than the simple *gîte d'étape* listed in the *Sentier de la Haute-Auvergne topo-guide*, but the *gîte* is actually part of the Hôtel du Bès, a very friendly little hotel by the river. My room was on the second floor and the shower lies just off the bar on the ground floor, which meant padding through the crowded bar in bare feet while swathed in a towel, but none of the locals seemed to mind, and the entire village was very interested in my walk which had been previewed in the local paper. Madame, who was doing the ironing while chatting to the customers, told me that as I was the only guest, and as she would be tired after doing the ironing, would I mind dining at the café across the road? The little café having a terrace above the river, bathed in the evening sun, I wouldn't mind a bit. That settled, she returned to the ironing and I went out for a look around.

St-Juéry was once a walled and fortified town, a frontier post between the Auvergne and the Gévaudan. Vestiges of the fortifications still remain, notably in remnants of the *enceinte and* the medieval tower of the village church which stand beside the old pack-horse bridge. The cross on the bridge over the Bès, which is now held together with wire hoops, is said to be the oldest cross in the Gévaudan and dates from the twelfth century. The whole place is pretty, the old houses built in gold- or silver-coloured stone, many with blue-tiled roofs, and there was the usual riot of flowers in all the window boxes. But the central and most unexpected gem of St-Juéry is the church. From the outside this looks ordinary enough, a simple, grey-stone building, but the inside is quite marvellous. This barrel-vaulted church is panelled from the floor to the top of the vault with fine-grained wood – it is rather like being inside an upturned boat. As I later learned, this exquisite panelling was the gift of the local foresters and carpenters after the church and much of the village had been burned by Waffen-SS troops from the Das Reich Division in 1944.

St-Juéry is a place not unaccustomed to horror, for this is one of the Gévaudan villages raided by that malevolent monster, the awesome Beast of the Gévaudan. When I heard all about this fabled creature, I was rather glad I slept within the safety of walls and not in some thin-skinned tent out on the lonely mountain. The story of the Beast begins in the last decades of the *Ancien Régime,* and the first incident can be quoted directly from a report by the local bishop in the autumn of 1745.

'La sus-dite Delphine Courtiol a été devorée dans son jardin, au dite lieu de Saint Juéry, par une bête féroce et inconnue quon prétend être hyena . . . .'

Whatever it was, the monster that tore poor Delphine to pieces in her garden by the river at St-Juéry was not a hyena and neither, as some said, was it a bear. From the month of August 1745, two decades before it struck elsewhere, the *Bête* ravaged the Gévaudan, and by the time Delphine met her end, it had already killed and eaten some sixty people, while many more had been attacked. The survivors reported a huge wolf – some said a werewolf. There were reports of further attacks in the Rouergue and further north in the Auvergne, and before long the whole countryside was so alarmed that no one went out after dark unless armed, and the Bishop of Mende ordered public prayers for the destruction of this monster which was preying on his flock.

Twenty years later the *Bête* was still active. Monsieur Ollier, the *curé* of L'Orcières, wrote: '*La Bête Féroce* has commenced his ravages in my parish in January 1765. On the 22nd, he ate a woman, aged twenty-five, in Chabandles, tearing off her head which was found two hundred paces from her body . . . the consternation was great at her funeral.' Sighs of relief went up from much of southern France when, in September 1765, a huge wolf was shot in the Bois de Pommier, on the Allier. The snag is that wolves do not behave like the *Bête du Gévaudan;* they are far from ferocious and hunt only in packs. The local hunters had killed scores of wolves in their hunt for the *Bête,* but the attacks continued for twenty years. Even then some said that it was no wolf that had done these things but a mad dog, perhaps one of those large Italian hunting dogs that the nobility imported from the Italian Abruzzi. Jean Chastel, the man who shot the great wolf in the Bois de Pommier, was himself a strange character, who had spent many years as a galley slave of the Moors, and had once been suspected of sorcery. It is said that he despatched the *Bête,* if it was the *Bête,* with a silver bullet which, as all know, is the only way to kill a werewolf. Certainly the attacks stopped, but the story of the *Bête du Gévaudan, la bête qui mangeait le monde,* is still discussed in the country districts of the Lozère as if the events of this strange story happened only yesterday.

Once the novelty of my presence had worn off, dinner that night was the usual enjoyable affair. I was soon joined at the table by one of those returning citizens of the Massif Central who was now spending a month in his home village after working the rest of the year in Paris, bringing with him his dog, a curious hyena-like monster, spotted grey and black, with large ears. This *bête*-like creature attracted a number of wary glances.

As is often the situation in France, the café was run by the wife while the husband practised another trade, in this case working as a stone-mason. Monsieur arrived halfway through dinner, covered in dust, and after a throat-clearing beer or two at the bar, came over to our table for a chat. Once again I was reminded that in France it is almost impossible to be alone for long.

'There is plenty of work for those who want to do it,' he said firmly. 'A lot of city people are now buying holiday homes here *maisons secondaires* – and all the houses need doing up, fresh stonework, new walls, whatever, all have to be built. It's hard work.' He held up a hand that was short of two fingers. 'One slip with the cutter and – zut! – you are hurt. But you know, with the bar here and the restaurant – and we have summer rooms to let my wife and I do all right. It's a good life here, especially for the children. We don't have drugs, we make our own fun, we have the fishing, we play *boules,* there is a little hunting. You must stay on, Monsieur, and tomorrow we can go fishing, or', hopefully, 'perhaps you would play a round of *boules* after dinner?'

My companion at dinner – and I never caught his name – was a typical *Auvergnat de Paris.* 'Yes, I own a bar. Half the barmen of Paris come from the Auvergne or Lozère. Barmen are now our biggest export. They went to Paris when it got hard here – during the *Belle Epoque* —you know, before the Great War, and there they opened bars or restaurants. All the great cafés of Paris were begun by Auvergnats . . . La Closérie de Lilas, Chez Lipp, Les Deux Magôts, Café Flore, all the famous places were owned by Auvergnats. Take Roger Cazes, who has just died. His father, Marcellin, went up to Paris from the Aubrac in 1904 and opened Chez Lipp, and the family has run it ever since. But we still like to come home again. However long I stay away, St-Juéry is my home, Monsieur. Tomorrow, if you have the time, we can go for a walk together and I'll show it to you.'

Fishing, *boules* or a little walk would have been fun but I had to get on. Next day I had another long distance to cover on a fresh footpath, all the way south for twenty miles or so to Aumont-Aubrac on the eastern side of the Aubrac plateau, on a winding section of the circular *Tour des Monts de l'Aubrac* footpath, I left St-Juéry just after eight, for people rise early hereabouts, and the *Sentier de la Haute-Auvergne* took me over the Bès and up the hill past a little chapel, then across the Bès again at Courbepeyre, and then south to Fournels and Ternes. Fournels, where I joined the Aubrac *sentier*, is a large, sprawling village with a fine château, set in quite hilly, wooded country, where the open fields and the lower slopes of the hills are threaded with streams and were then completely carpeted with yellow daffodils, a glorious sight. I stopped a farmer to ask how these daffodils managed to survive in an age of intensive farming, a question which seemed to surprise him.

'The cows are not yet in the fields to tread on them, and of course we don't plough them up. Why should we not keep them, aren't they beautiful?' Indeed they are. Spring was in full flower here in the Gévaudan, the cuckoo was calling from every wood and the sky above was full of swallows, some of them swooping down and flitting past me at knee-height. The sky was blue, the clouds high – it was glorious.

South of Ternes, the *Tour des Monts de l'Aubrac* starts to climb steadily towards the high Aubrac and, once past the Truc de l'Homme at 4,090 feet, enters the Peyre country, of which little Courbepeyre is but the outpost. The heart of Peyre country lies mainly to the east of the Aubrac, running from Ste-Colombe-de-Peyre to St-Léger-de-Peyre, near Marvejols, with the 3,867-foot-high Roc de Peyre. This once supported the castle of the Lords of Peyre, a distinct landmark I would pass next day on my way south. Under the *Ancien Régime* the Peyre was one of the eight baronies of the Gévaudan, and the most powerful after that of d'Apcher. On this bright day, I lunched at a busy hotel in the village of Fau-de-Peyre, which has a magnificent church with one of those open Auvergne belfries where, to help the bell-ringers, the tower was provided with an exterior flight of steps. From Fau I walked out to Nozières, down the valley of the River Rimeize, which was a very beautiful route but over supplied with yet more of those truculent Auvergne cattle. Browsing through the *Tour des Monts de l'Aubrac topo-guide,* I had read that one way to upset these half-wild beasts, was to come between the *vache* and her *veau.* The guide was somewhat reticent on how this situation might be avoided, which was a matter of some regret as, coming round a corner, I found the GR footpath running between a surly bunch of *vaches* on the hill to my left and their *veaux* grazing on the riverbank to my right. After a little pondering (am I a man or a mouse?), I walked on down the path between them, flourishing my stick. But, as with that business between Albert and the Lion, you could see that the *vaches* didn't like it. As I half-ran through the gap, they shot down the slope behind me, horns clicking, and came skidding to a stop by the path, kicking up a cloud of dust and bellowing angrily. Luckily there was a stout fence ahead, which I went over with an impressive amount of agility for my age and, after a long, beautiful, and not entirely uneventful day's walk, I came at last to the Aubrac, one of my favourite parts of France.

It must be clear by now that I appreciate wide open spaces, prairie rather than forest, and prefer to walk on ridged downland rather than across mountains. I enjoy spacious, rolling land where the horizon keeps shifting away and where every hilltop offers a fresh view. If that land is empty of people – or at least tourists and full of history, so much the better. I don't think I am all that hard to please, but nowhere in the world do all my requirements come together quite as neatly as they do here in the Aubrac.

The Aubrac plateau (the term '*Monts*' is an exaggeration) is the most southerly of all the Auvergne plateaux created by volcanic action. It is a wide, rolling, rocky plain, quite thickly forested in the east, the section I had covered on this *sentier*. It opens out further west, before the little town of Nasbinals, and then grows even wider once past the central village of Aubrac. There it drops away sharply south, into the valley of the Lot. It is pasture land, full of sheep and cattle, a place where large fields are divided by stone walls, a country of streams and flowers, very lonely, very beautiful. I have crossed the Aubrac in every season of the year, on foot, on my bicycle, or on langlauf skis, and this high, wild land has never disappointed me, but never does it look as beautiful as it does in the early spring. Most of the Aubrac lies at about 3,000 feet above sea level. Here, open to all the winds that blow, the weather is both changeable and, on occasions, deadly. I have seen blizzards in the Aubrac in June, and there was still plenty of snow lying about under the trees as I marched south to Aumont on this warm afternoon in April, when weather and scenery combined to build the perfect day.

As to that other element, history, the Aubrac is full of it. The *département* straddles the old Compostela pilgrim road from Le Puy in the Vélay, 70 miles east across the Margeride. If you follow that old track west for a thousand miles or so, it leads to the city of Santiago de Compostela, 'the good city of the Apostle, which has in its keeping the precious mortal relics of St James, and is therefore considered the most fortunate, and the most exalted, of all the cities of Spain', as the twelfth-century monk and traveller, Ameri Picaud, puts it in his *Liber Sancti Jacobi* which, among other things, is one of the world's first guidebooks. This particular Road to Compostela, which is one of four which lead across France to the Pyrenees, was pioneered by Bishop Goshalk of Le Puy in 951 AD, only a hundred years or so after the relics of St James were discovered at the *Campo-Stellae, the* Field of Stars, on the coast of Spanish Galicia. That journey by Bishop Goshalk began the Santiago pilgrimage, which reached its peak in the twelfth and thirteenth centuries and flourishes to this day.

Come to the Aubrac at the end of June, any time from the middle of the month on, and you will see the Compostela pilgrims heading west, on foot, by car or on bicycles, all aiming to reach the city of St James by St James's Day, 25 July. You can spot them easily, for all carry a scallop-shell, *la coquille de St Jacques,* the emblem of St James. The pilgrim road from Le Puy is the most picturesque and difficult of all the routes, and it leads to many of the most famous pilgrim places, notably the Abbey Church of Conques in the Rouergue, and the village of Aubrac, out on the Aubrac plateau.

Aubrac lies on the GR65, the *Chemin de St Jacques* footpath, one of the longest GR trails and one that follows, as far as possible, the traces of the old pilgrim route. In the year 1120, Adelard, Count of Flanders, was on his way to Compostela when he was attacked by robbers on the Aubrac plateau and, when crossing it again on his way home, found himself lost in a thick mist. To prevent such incidents happening to other pilgrims and for the honour of his house and St James, Adelard built a hospice in the middle of this gaunt plateau, '*en loco horroris et vastae solitudinis*', as a sign on the church at Aubrac puts it, and endowed his foundation with funds to support a body of soldier-monks, charging them with the task of protecting pilgrims on the Way of St James. In the tower of the church he installed a great bell called *La Maria, la cloche des perdus,* The Bell of the Lost, which the monks would toll whenever the mist clamped down in the hills, a sound which must have guided many wanderers to safety over the centuries. The pilgrim road enters the Aubrac at Aumont and heads west across the plateau through Malbuzon and Nasbinals into Aubrac and continues down to the Lot valley, a route which is well worth following, even all the way to Spain.

Early in the year, little Aubrac dreams away the springtime days, waiting for the annual influx of pilgrims. The monks have gone and the great tower, erected to protect the inhabitants against the English *routiers* during the Hundred Years War, and therefore called the *Tour des Anglais,* is now simply a *gîte d'étape.* But the old pilgrim path can still be traced across the nearby hills and, apart from the motor cars swishing along the main road, little else has changed hereabouts in the last thousand years. On all my journeys across this *loco vastae* – which may be vast but is far from horrible – I have stopped for lunch at Aubrac, after a night stop at my favourite hotel in all France, the Grande Hôtel de la Gare, Chez Prouhèze, in Aumont, to which my dusty boots were now transporting me at an impressive pace and, as I blundered in through the front door, Guy and Catherine Prouhèze were waiting to greet me.

I've known the Prouhèze family for quite a few years and although I never mention the Aubrac – and I mention it a lot – without putting in a word for their hotel, I sometimes wonder why they put up with me. Their hotel is elegant and not inexpensive, their restaurant has a Michelin rosette, and their clientèle is *chic* as only a French clientèle can be – and then there is me. I come to the Aubrac to revel in the wild, and the first time I entered the Hôtel Prouhèze it was on all fours and covered in snow. That caused a certain *frisson* among the other guests. On the next occasion, I had forgotten where the hotel was, came upon it suddenly, swerved off the road into the station forecourt, braked, skidded on the gravel and crashed into the wall of the *gare*. That did not go down too well either. Some years later, after seventy miles on a bicycle from Le Puy, my arrival in their grand dining room on a Friday evening in June didn't add much elegance to the setting, but they let that pass. The Prouhèzes always seem pleased to see me and on this occasion, they were more than willing, indeed eager, to help on the Trans-France walk.

On our original programme, Geoff was to rejoin me here, and come with me on the last section to the sea, leaving his car here in Guy's care. With Aumont lying on the main railway line, we could take the train back up from Montpellier to collect it after finishing the walk. My first task on arrival, therefore, was to explain what had happened to Geoff. He had become locked into yet another rugby event (some people never learn), and would now join me three days hence on the Tarn. What we would then do with his car was a problem we could leave for another day. Meanwhile I fancied yet another *kir-royale*, a hot bath and then a long evening in the restaurant, where Guy's cooking was complemented by the wines on Catherine's list which she had chosen, it said here, '*avec l'aimable complicité de Georges Aoust*'. Bearing in mind that some of these wines cost up to L200 a bottle, I think this *complicité* needs watching. Any evening spent relishing such dishes as *fillet de truite aux ravioles et bouillon de légumes crémé la ciboulette*, has to be enjoyable, even if, like me, you stick to the Fr150 menu.

Running a top-class French restaurant isn't easy, as Guy never ceases to assure me. 'First you have to be good, then people have to know you're good, then you have to stay good. Even if no one comes – and in winter, sometimes, no one comes; you know, *cher Rob*, what the weather can be like here . . . but still you need the finest wines, sauces, fresh flowers on the tables . . . what if the one customer is the Michelin inspector, eh? And the customers, they are very *exigeants* . . . yes, demanding.'

So they are, and so they should be. It is my not-so-secret belief that the real reason for the general excellence of French restaurants is the high standards demanded by the clientèle. Alas, the French too are getting lax and it is now harder than it once was to get a really memorable meal in France. It must also be said that once a place becomes infested by the British, standards usually plummet. I recall tackling the owner of one hotel in Normandy on this very point, and his answer was quite blunt. 'We can cook good food, Monsieur, but most of our clients are English, and they won't eat it . . . so don't blame me.'

I only hope that this little *histoire* does not lead too many of *les Anglais* to the Hôtel Prouhèze, or if it does, that they go there on foot. I spent a very pleasant evening at the hotel, basking modestly in the admiration of the other guests, who were gratifyingly impressed that I had come so far on foot across France. Then, before going to bed, I slipped out for a walk. It was again bitterly cold, with a keen wind sweeping down from the north, promising a clear, hot day for the morrow. I still had about two hundred miles to go, and the weather was going to get warmer as I neared the sea, but I left that problem for the morning and went to bed.

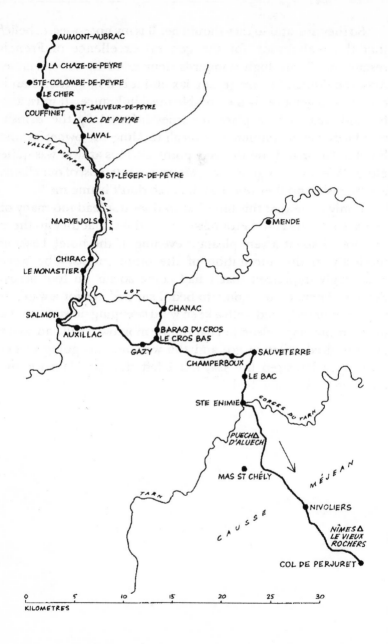

CHAPTER NINE

CROSSING THE CAUSSE COUNTRY

'The grand object of travel is to see the
shores of the Mediterranean.'
Dr. Johnson

I left the Grande Hôtel de la Gare in Aumont at my usual early
hour, first wandering back into the centre of the town to find
a bank. It was now Friday and another three days might
elapse before I could again lay my hands on some cash. Besides,
I had a hangover. As expected, this was one of those clear, bright,
Aubrac mornings, when the weather could go either way, a sharp,
blue sky promising much in the east, but large, black-bellied
clouds scudding in a threatening fashion across the low wooded
hills to the west. I decided to make as much distance as possible
down the trail before the weather had time to make up its mind
and, having said goodbye to Guy and Catherine, I was plodding
up the hill out of the town before nine o'clock.

The path out of Aumont follows the route of the GR65 (*Le
Chemin de St Jacques*) for a while, along the line of the Roman *Via
Agrippa,* which once ran across France from Lyon to Bordeaux.
You have to know and believe in the existence of the Roman road
hereabouts, because there are no signs, no stones grooved by
chariot wheels, no indication at all of Romans passing. The path
circles south-west out of Aumont, towards the open Aubrac, and
comes out of the woods by La Chaze-de-Peyre, crossing a stream
into another wood, and then leaves Ste-Colombe-de-Peyre to the
west, and points south for Le Cher. There was plenty of snow

lying under the trees and I had to walk fast simply to stay warm, but rapid progress soon brought me to Couffinet. This section took me about an hour, which gave me time to ponder my next course of action.

The errant Geoff was now aiming to rejoin me at St Enimie on the Tarn which, compared with the miles already covered, was no great distance away, and I had three full days to get there. I could therefore afford to slow my pace a little, or stray off my southern path for some other route – or maybe even take half a day off. On the other hand, the sun was getting hot, the country ahead more and more barren. I already knew that the terrain would become increasingly jagged as I marched towards the Tarn, while beyond that lay the wild and steep hills of the Cévennes, where careful map reading was advisable. Most of my maps were still that small 1:100,000 scale, which are far from ideal in close mountain country or on open, featureless plateaux. The snag was that none of the village shops I had visited so far stocked many maps at all, and none had maps for anywhere outside their immediate local area. Clearly I needed a town, and the only town within a day's march of the Aubrac was the fortress town of Marvejols. I dumped the pack off my shoulders on to the ground with a heavy thud and sat on it to consider my options, eventually deciding that as I could follow my next footpath, the GR60, for a long way later on, I could afford to veer off it for a while and head south across the Peyre country to Marvejols for some serious map-shopping. This decided, I left the GR *Tour des Monts de l'Aubrac* at Le Cher, heading on a compass bearing for Couffinet, walking easily through lightly wooded country.

Couffinet is just a hamlet beside the main N9 road, but from there a track, which soon becomes a single footpath, leads up to St-Sauveur-de-Peyre, a large, sprawling village just north of the outcrop of the Roc de Peyre, a mound which once supported the Lord of Peyre's castle but now has a way up and a *table d'orientation* on top. From up there, the Peyre country lies open on every side;

to the north I could still see those long-promised peaks of the Plomb du Cantal which I had crossed so painfully five days before, the tops now etched in black and white against the blue sky; to the west lay the long slopes of the Aubrac, also dappled with snow, while to the south I could see the flat-topped outcrops of the southern *causse* country. The weather had clearly decided to turn benign, and it was very hot indeed by midday as I trudged south to the village of Laval before descending a steep hill towards the river and the railway line which runs through the Vallée d'Enfer, Hell-Valley, and south towards Marvejols.

From Laval the road winds on and on down the steep-sided Val d'Enfer, through a typically wild, beautiful and remote place of the Gévaudan, the valley plunging deeply between high cliffs cloaked in golden gorse and, as usual, completely devoid of people. No cattle grazed on the upper slopes, the occasional *buron* or farmhouse was either deserted or in ruins, and no cars came past during that long descent from the high plateau, down a minor road littered with large rocks which had fallen from the sheer cliffs above.

Here and there the French had erected their usual 'Beware of falling rocks' road signs, but while I take the point, I have never quite seen what the person passing below such cliffs is supposed to do about rockfalls. If a rock comes whistling down onto your head or car-roof, it is hardly likely you would hear it in time to take avoiding action. However, I did pay a little more attention when passing one spot where a rock the size of a dustbin lay plumb in the centre of the road. These rockfalls are most common after heavy rain, which loosens rocks from the soil – or when, as today, the weather warms up at the end of winter. During the winter months, water seeps into the rockface crevasses, freezes into ice, expands, and thereby loosens the rock which is easily dislodged when the ice melts. Add heavy rain or some high winds to this mix and ice-loosened rocks can fall on the road below like hailstones from mid-morning on, so it pays to be a little cautious and stick close to the rockface when passing underneath a cliff.

This minor road, the D2, winds down to St-Léger-de-Peyre, past the outskirts of *Le Parc Zoologique du Gévaudan*, where various examples of the local fauna, and other, now rare European animals, including wolves, bears and bison, are kept as a tourist attraction. St-Léger is a rather tumbledown village which straggles up a valley to the east, and because the only bar in striking distance was closed, I had no option but to press on into Marvejols, where I arrived limping badly from too much road-walking, at the end of a sunny afternoon, having covered a distance of some twenty miles.

Marvejols is a rather splendid medieval town, with huge, high, fortified gates to the north, south and west. The only distractions from a favourable first impression are two bronze statues by the gates, one in the *Place des Cordeliers* to the slayer of the *Bête du Gévaudan,* and another, even worse, of that mighty monarch, Henri IV of France and Navarre. This last statue stands by the northern gate, *La Porte de Soubeyran.* I will not rave on about this awful figure, which is half life-sized and resembles a pantomime dwarf, but since Henri of Navarre is one of my heroes, who rebuilt the town after it was burnt by the Holy Catholic League in 1586, I feel he deserves something a lot better than this. That apart, Marvejols is a pretty place, reeking of history.

During the first part of the Hundred Years War, Marvejols was a base for the Constable of France, Bertrand du Guescelin, in his attempts to drive the English out of the Auvergne, and suppress *the routiers* of the Free Companies. These Anglo-French wars finally ended in 1453 when the English were defeated at Castillon in the Dordogne, but a hundred years later France was again gripped by civil war, the so-called Wars of Religion, between the Protestant Huguenots and the forces of the Catholic League, headed by Henri III of France for the Catholics, and his heir, the Protestant Henri of Navarre for the Huguenots. Henri of

Navarre is best remembered for his gallantry, his love-life, his white plume, his *sauce béarnaise* (although this was actually invented much later), and for two remarks: that 'Paris is worth a Mass', when he accepted the fact that he could gain the throne of France only as a Catholic; and the comment that he wished to bring his kingdom to such prosperity that every peasant, however poor, 'might have a chicken for his dinner *(une poule au pot)* every Sunday'. Henri was a terrible cynic, and a great opportunist, but his heart was in the right place and his courage unquestioned.

In the 1580s, when his fortunes hung in the balance, the King's Army in the Auvergne and Gévaudan was led by the fanatic Duc de Joyeuse. In 1586 Joyeuse captured the castle on the Roc de Peyre, reducing the walls to dust with his cannon, then moved against the Protestant stronghold of Marvejols, which fell by assault and was put to the torch. In 1588, Joyeuse was killed at the battle of Coutras, north of the Dordogne, when Henri swept away the Catholic field army with one cavalry charge. After Henri became King of France, he ordered that Marvejol should be rebuilt and the King's statue by the *Porte de Soubeyran* was erected much later to commemorate his generosity.

Now nominally Catholic, Henri IV remained loyal to his Protestant supporters, attempting to ensure their safety and their rights to religious freedom by the Edict of Nantes, which he issued in 1598. This guaranteed the Protestants the right to practise their religion, though not to preach it to others, and guaranteed them certain areas to control and places of security. These rights were gradually whittled away by Louis XIII and Cardinal Richelieu, and taken away completely when Louis XIV published *The Revocation of the Edict of Nantes* in 1685. Denied the right to practise their religion, many Huguenots fled abroad, a goodly number to England, but here in the south of France, the Protestant people are of stubborn stock and they began a war in the Cévennes which smouldered on for a hundred years, from 1687 until the outbreak of the French Revolution – but more of that later. For the moment, here I was, resting in Marvejols on a warm late-April evening, watching the crowds mill about in the narrow cobbled streets, finding most of the maps I needed in the *Maison de la Presse,* and chatting to the local correspondent of *Midi-Libre,* who had come up from Mende to see me. All in all, a good end to a rather pleasant, useful day.

Where the terrain looked tricky and where I could find them, I bought the 1:25,000 maps, but although such detailed mapping was really necessary only now and again, there were good reasons for relying more or less on the 1:100,000 versions – not least those of cost and weight. It takes just seventy-four sheets of the 1:100,000 scale to cover all of France, but it needs eleven hundred of the 1:50,000, and an impressive two thousand sheets to blanket France on the 1:25,000. Even in France, the 1:25,000 cost around £4 a sheet. I needed nine 1:100,000 maps to cross France, plus *topo-guides,* and some 1:25,000 maps for the mountain sections. Together with a compass and a little guesswork, they got me to my destination in the end.

I am very much against walking down metalled roads of any description, especially the traffic-crammed main route variety, but there have to be exceptions. I left Marvejols early in the day, while it was still cool, hurrying down the N9, first passing Chirac, a fine old village with a beautiful Romanesque church, and then through Le Monastier, which has a church restored by Pope Urban V in the twelfth century. From there I sped along, down to where the Colagne joins the great River Lot near Moriès, and was sitting in the little café by the bridge at Port de Salmon just in time for an early lunch, having lopped off a useful amount of distance. The small Causse de Villard rose up on the east, and my path, the GR60, led to the great Causse de Sauveterre across the bridge to my right. The Causse itself was hidden by the trees rising on the far side of the Lot, but I knew it was there and was looking foward to walking across it. I love the *causse* country.

A *causse* is a plateau, and the *causses* are the great and most noticeable physical feature of the country south of the Massif Central, between those central mountains and the Languedoc plain. They are the result of the upheaval which created the Massif Central, heaving all the land up to the 3,000-foot mark, to a height where the air is chill and the winds fierce. Since then erosion down the millenia has cut great river valleys through the high plateau, so that the once complete *causse* country is now divided by rivers, deep green slashes through the otherwise barren uplands. There are plenty of *causses*, large, medium and small in southern France, and my route south on the GR60 footpath lay across two of the finest of the *Grandes Causses, the* Causse de Sauveterre, between the Lot and the Tarn, and the Causse Méjean, which divides the Tarn from the Jonte. Beyond that lay my final obstacle, the Cévennes, and my route across those hills followed the *Grande Draille du Languedoc,* now the GR60, one of the great footpaths of France. These *drailles,* or drove roads, are not uncommon in southern Languedoc, and have been used since ancient times by drovers or shepherds to take their sheep or cattle from winter shelter in the valleys up to summer grazing on the high, wild *causses*. Although this practice has nearly ceased, the roads remain clearly marked as grooves across the land – the perfect route for walkers.

As a lover of open country, I like the *causses*. They are, in effect, deserts – at least in the sense that they are open, barren, stony, and virtually treeless. They can also be quite outstandingly bleak if the weather is other than fine. Best of all though, they are lonely. As they lie at the 3,000-foot mark, my first task after crossing the Lot – which passes below the Pont de Salmon at about 1,312 feet – was to plod uphill to the *causse,* walking for hour after hour under a blazing sun, through the little village of Auxillac, which lay like a dream in golden stone, all picked out with blood-red geraniums. This uphill walk gives wide, misty views back to the Aubrac, and many chances to pause on the way up to the open high lands. I found it necessary to stop frequently, panting for water but enjoying the views, which are simply breathtaking.

Walking north to south across this rugged country had been one of the aims of my trip, for here as nowhere else, even in France, I get that sense of solitude. It is a sensation which is quite different from, and much more pleasant than, loneliness. The GR60 path ran on across the *causse,* a lighter line traced among the flat stones, with buzzards hanging overhead, soaring on the hot air currents, while skylarks sang in the thorn scrub, and the open country was ablaze with spring flowers. Here and there a deep green patch stood out, a place where all the stones had been laboriously cleared away to make a small pasture – a *sotch.* There is very little water in the *causses* but there is dew, which is collected in *lavognes,* or dewponds, to water the sheep, and if the stones are cleared away crops will grow here. But the labour needed to create a *sotch* must be tremendous, for the piles of stones cleared from some of these small pastures reached as high as a pyramid. To grow any commercial crop would therefore be exceptionally difficult, and for the most part this is sheep and goat pasture land. Goats will live on almost anything and the sheep somehow get by on the sparse vegetation. Barren though they are, then, the *causses* do support a small community of farmers and shepherds, and by mid-afternoon I was anxious to find one of these farms because I had finished all my water and was very, very thirsty.

Gazy, where I arrived about five o'clock, has long been abandoned by its original inhabitants and has been taken over by people from the surrounding towns who have purchased and rebuilt the peasant houses as *Maisons secondaires,* so there was much rebuilding in progress and the steady hum of lawnmowers, a noise which ceased as I arrived and everyone came out to stare, and promptly started up again after I had passed through. The man who filled my water-bottle did so with great reluctance, but at Le Cros Bas, further on, I imposed upon a farmer for more water and, like all true country people, he was much more friendly, even inviting me in for a rest and a glass of wine before showing me my way off the GR60, out onto the main road at Baraq du Cros, from where I plodded downhill into Chanac.

Chanac turned out to be much bigger and much nicer than I had imagined from the map. The staff at the Hôtel des Voyageurs made me very welcome, the guests at a wedding reception sent me a chilled glass of Champagne, and after that I took off to explore the old streets, the church and the castle before returning to the hotel for dinner. On the television news, the *météo* forecast for the next few days looked quite promising – low winds, moderate heat, no rain; perfect for my purpose. I even polished my thorn-scratched boots before going to bed, and slept like a log until daylight.

The walk uphill, and back to the Causse de Sauveterre next morning was actually rather pleasant. The weather was beautiful and, providing the gradient is gentle, I would always much rather go up than down. There were, however, snags. just past Le Cros Bas I came to a house where the garden was full of cages and each cage was full of hounds of every shape, size and variety. All of them went collectively mad at the sight of me. One hound even managed to howl while doing standing four-legged jumps up to the roof of its cage and, after a day 'excused dogs' on the empty *causse*, I was soon heartily sick of their clamour. It followed me for half an hour as I, in turn, pursued the winding GR60 path through the pines and back out onto the bare plateau.

Heading south-east from Chanac, the GR60, here the *Grande Draille d'Aubrac*, angles around the *causse*, to the village of Champerboux. This, like so many of these villages, is tucked away in a fold of the hills and grows as you come upon it, turning swiftly from a single roof and steeple into a considerable village. But alas, this village was one without a bar, a situation which had come to represent a minor tragedy. Two or three hours walking in the wild seem ample justification for a glass of water, and (better still) a *demi-pression* and in my, by now extensive, experience of small French villages, any village with a church was sure to have a bar – except, that is, Champerboux. Even the standpipe for water outside the church turned out to be dry, and I was once again very thirsty. My problem was solved by an elderly lady from a nearby house who came out with a glass and a jug of crystal clear, chill water, which I gulped down with the alacrity of a camel. I then got lost.

This might be as good a time as any to explain why someone who claims to have some little experience of travel in the great outdoors seems to have the propensity for getting thirsty and getting lost. What is experience worth if you still make basic mistakes? My answer is quite simple – 'experienced' is just another way of describing someone who makes mistakes and gets away with them. Someone else said that experience consists of one year learning the rules and thirty years breaking them, and I simply don't worry about problems until they appear. Life is too short to spend it anticipating situations and difficulties that may never occur – and which sometimes occur anyway, whether you anticipate them or not. I can follow the rules and the waymarks, but if the waymarks peter out, I will get lost. I can carry water which staves off thirst for a while, but I can't carry enough to stave it off forever, so I get thirsty. On the road to Compostela I set off each morning with two litres of water on the bike, but was often crawling around in the dust by mid-afternoon, because the temperature sometimes soared to 46°C (115°F) in the shade, and there is no shade on the Pilgrim Road across Navarre. It is much easier to make a small error and claw back from it, than to spend time, which could be more pleasantly employed, in anticipating situations that might never arise. The problem here at Champerboux was caused by the junction of two footpaths.

The GR44 swings in from the east to join the GR60 briefly at Champerboux and, through some inattention, I found myself heading east along the GR44, rather than south on the GR60. I continued to climb out of the village heading in the wrong direction, until I hit a metalled road, which brought me to my senses. Judging from the map, no metalled road crossed my route, so where was I? About here, I guessed, near the village of Sauveterre. I therefore got out the compass, set 180° on it and cut due south across the *causse*, to rejoin the GR60 just above Le Bac. There the path falls off the Causse de Sauveterre down towards Ste Enimie, in the deep, green gorges of the Tarn, which were now looming mistily ahead of me. Getting back on to track took less than an hour – easy.

According to the road signs there was still another five miles of road-walking before Ste Enimie. This clashed with the information in the GR60 *topo-guide*, but the difference was soon explained by the fact that while the metalled road winds to and fro along the sides of the gorge and loses height to the river only slowly, the GR footpath drops down on to the old *draille* road which predates the motor-car and simply heads steeply down into Ste Enimie – that most delightful of Tarn-side towns – and arrives at the river after leading through the narrow, cobbled backstreets of the town. It was just after two in the afternoon, and my day's stage had already been completed.

The gorges of the River Tarn are one of the great natural wonders of France. They run east-west for nearly thirty miles across Lozère, between Florac and Le Rozier, cutting deeply into a fissure of the *causse*, the base touching a depth of around 400 feet below the natural level of the plateau. Down in that steep-sided, sheltered valley, a little micro-climate exists, creating a place much greener, cooler and more gentle than up on the barren *causse*. It is a valley where small towns and villages can shelter among peach and apple orchards, the old houses draped in blossom and great drifts of wisteria, and set below soaring cliffs picked out in red and ochre. If you wish to visit a spectacular spot in France, then come south to these rugged gorges of the Tarn.

Ste Enimie lies at the most northern tip of the Tarn gorges, at the point where the river turns south under the great high bridge and flows past the Château de la Caze and La Malène, through the narrows at Les Détroits, and so down to the exit of the gorges at Le Rozier. East of Ste Enimie lies the castle at Castelbouc, and the twin villages of Quézac and Ispagnac. It is here the gorges really begin, creating a thirty-mile sweep of river and mountain which combine to form the most attractive and dramatic scenery I had encountered so far on my walk. The whole of it soared into view from the old *draille* road as I walked in off the northern *causse*.

Quite apart from the setting, Ste Enimie is a pretty spot, an old town which dates back to Merovingian times when, so it is said, this little corner of the valley contained a miraculous healing spring. To this spot came a Merovingian princess, Enimie, the daughter of King Clotaire and the sister of King Dagobert. She was taking refuge from her brother, who wished to marry her off to one of his more powerful and recalcitrant barons. Princess Enimie wished only to devote her life to prayer, but he insisted on the marriage. When she was dragged away for the wedding, she was immediately smitten with leprosy, which ravaged her face until she was allowed to return to her cell by the river. There, her sores washed by the waters from the spring, she quickly recovered, but when her brother took her away again, the leprosy promptly returned. Finally she was allowed to stay in peace by the river and, as Ste Enimie, she spent the rest of her fife setting a good example to the wild folk who lived beside the Tarn. Today, like so many pilgrim places, little Ste Enimie is a tourist town and a popular spot for motorists touring the gorges of the Tarn, but the Church of Ste Enimie can still be visited. There is also an abbey and the relics of old fortifications, while the whole place – town and situation – is quite beautiful. I spent a very contented afternoon in Ste Enimie, sitting in the sun on the riverbank and bathing my feet in the chilly waters of the Tarn, while awaiting the arrival of an old friend, Guy Rouffiac, from Mende.

When Geoff found he could not join me at Aumont, we had arranged to meet at the *logis* in Ste Enimie, but the discovery that the *logis* would be shut, forced us to change our plans to a meeting in Ste Enimie, from which we would drive to the nearest *logis* at Mende. From there Geoff could deliver me back to the footpath at Ste Enimie next morning. Then it transpired that Geoff might not reach Ste Enimie by a respectable hour, so we arranged to meet in the hotel in Mende. To get me from Ste Enimie to Mende I needed a lift, and hence the help of Guy Rouffiac, who turned up promptly at five, and bore me off to my night stop.

On our drive across the *causse* to Mende, we passed a fortified farmhouse at Le Choizal, and I heard a little more about the region's problem for which, here as elsewhere, tourism is seen as part of the answer.

'We have the Common Market Agricultural Policy, which helps, but as you can see . . .,' Guy gestured out of the window at the stony, barren countryside, 'this land isn't very fertile. Most of the farms need to cultivate three hundred – maybe five hundred hectares, just to scratch a living. But we survive. I wouldn't live anywhere else – and I notice you keep coming back.'

I met Guy years ago on that ski trip to the Aubrac when the guide tried to show us the Plomb du Cantal, and when that still-wild area was even wilder than it is today. One day he took me to lunch at his family's farm where his mother was full of questions about the Royal Family, and somewhat disappointed to find that I didn't know any of them personally. Guy runs the Tourist Office in Mende, the present capital of Lozère, and as such he has been called on several times over the years, on those occasions when I had either been simply passing by, or had, as on the Robert Louis Stevenson Walk, bitten off rather more than I could chew, and needed his help or a lift. Since Mende is a very agreeable town and the Hôtel du Pont de Roupt an agreeable hotel, a night there seemed an excellent idea. But when we arrived – no Geoff.

There was still no sign of Geoff at seven, or at eight, or at nine, and by ten o'clock that night, knowing what I did of Geoff's driving, I was worried. Just before panic set in, the phone finally rang.

'Where the hell are you?'

Geoff sounded weary. 'I'm at Châtillon-sur-Indre.'

'Where!? What? That's bloody miles away. How in the . . . ?'

'I know . . . don't nag . . . the traffic is terrible and I missed the boat . . . now don't get mad at me. I'll join you tomorrow.'

Actually, I was rather relieved, and we arranged to meet next day some time in the evening, on the Col de Perjuret, south of the Causse Méjean. With that settled and a load off my mind, I finally went to bed.

Next morning Guy returned me to Ste Enimie by 10 a.m. My departure from there, however, was a little delayed by an encounter with the Mayor, who led me to his parlour and presented me with yet another heavy press kit. It was almost mid-morning before I was on the south side of the Tarn gorge, climbing up the steep, winding path that took an hour and a half to deliver me to *the causse* at the top. Seen from the river, the sides of the gorge soar up front and back – it is much more than a gorge, the word is inadequate; it is a canyon, which would not look out of place in the Rockies. At the bottom, the thought of flogging up that sheer-sided cliff was quite daunting, but I had learned a bit about cliff-climbing by now and you do it, as I did the whole journey, one step at a time. Taken like that, pausing now and again for a pant, sweat dripping onto the stones by my boots, I climbed on steadily, up and up to the breezy top of the gorge, where the poorly waymarked path finally reaches the Causse Méjean and heads south past the Puech – or hill – d'Aluech, and south across a terrain which is as barren as that of the Causse de Sauveterre, but much more hilly. Here the *Draille d'Aubrac* is known as the *Grande Draille du Languedoc* and is popular with horsemen and trail-riders. I met several groups of riders who all stopped for a chat. These encounters broke up the journey as I walked all day over rolling country, past the *gîte d'étape* at the Mas St-Chély which was another reminder that I was getting well south, *mas* being a Languedoc word – then past the glider-drome on the open grassland of the Plaine de Chanet and, just too late for lunch, into the little village of Nivoliers. To my surprise and delight this had a bar, a restaurant-hotel and yet another *gîte*, into which I fell for a cold beer and half an hour out of my boots. Having the rest of the day to reach the Col de Perjuret and my rendezvous with Geoff, I was in no great hurry to leave this wonderful, wild *causse* country.

A rest in that beautiful little spot put wings on my heels. Another couple of hours' walking across the rolling *causse*, past the rock chaos called Nîmes-le-Vieux, heading directly now towards the tall radio masts on what must be Mont Aigoual, the high point of the Cévennes, delivered me to the Col de Perjuret by five in the evening. I lay in the long grass by the road for a while, looking north-east across the valley to the spectacular high cliffs at the point where the road over the *col* plunged away towards Florac – but still no Geoff. I waited there for nearly an hour, while the sun swung down to the west – and still no Geoff. Eventually, I went to the telephone box which stands at the summit of the *col*. This being France, it was working, and I phoned the Hôtel du Pont de Roupt. Yes, they said, Geoff had finally arrived to collect my rucksack, but he had left there only an hour before. Even so, given the way Geoff drives, it would not take him long, and I had hardly returned to the *col* when I saw his car far below, speeding up the winding road from Florac. Finally it swung off on to the verge and braked beside me in a cloud of dust.

'That,' he said, jerking his thumb back at the void behind, 'is the closest you can get to hang-gliding with your wheels still on the ground. But here I am . . . and I don't want to hear a word out of you.'

'I'll only say that I did spend months telling everyone how organised and reliable you are. Yet so far on this trip you are averaging two days late at every rendezvous.'

When I finally got the truth out of him, Geoff's reputation as the super-planner took a further knock. Having booked his passage back to Ouistreham on Saturday night, he had failed to notice that that was the one day in the year when the boat sailed at three in the afternoon, and was therefore down at the rugby club when he should have been boarding the ferry. Frantic rearranging by Toby Oliver's staff got him to Ouistreham twenty-four hours later.

The boot of Geoff's car was an Aladdin's cave, full of good things – like half-bottles of Scotch – and after half an hour spent crawling through the duty-frees in celebration of our reunion, I climbed into the car and we drove up to the observatory and viewpoint on the top of Mont Aigoual, just six miles to the south. There I discovered, as usual, that my legs had seized up, and by the time I had creaked out of the car to limp to the top, Geoff had already been up to the crest and was walking back towards me, smiling, jerking his thumb over his shoulder.

'You just come and have a look at this,' he said, grabbing me by the arm. 'It's a sight for sore feet.'

He led me to the edge of the escarpment, to the point where the chill evening wind came rushing over the crest, soughing through the frame of the radio mast above. He pointed south.

'Look at that!'

'I'm looking. What am I looking at?'

'There. Use your eyes.'

By now it was seven in the evening, a cold and clear evening, one of those beautiful, still evenings when the green hills of the Cévennes rippled away into the far distance, with each green ridge divided from the next by a misty blue valley and the whole landscape mellowed by the evening sun as far as the eye could see.

'Look there,' said Geoff again, pointing. 'Away on the far horizon, as far as your eyes will take you . . . at that blue streak.'

'I can see it,' I said, shading my eyes, 'but what is it?'

'It's the sea,' said Geoff.

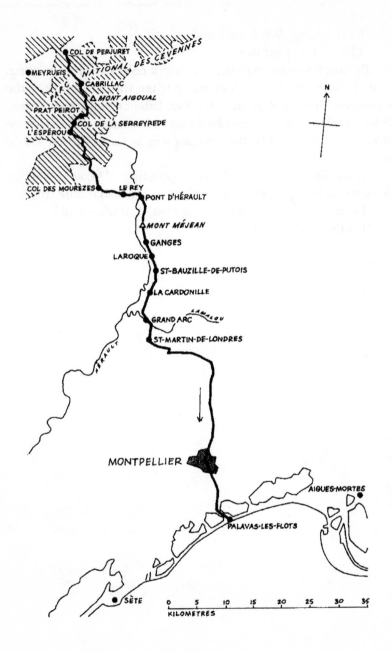

CHAPTER TEN

CEVENNES AND GARRIGUE

'The only reward of a thing well done is to have done it.'
Emerson

The sea – that was a major step in the right direction! The sea was in sight at long last, but there remained eighty very up-and-down miles between our chilly mountain top and the warm Mediterranean. I have walked across the Cévennes before, and although it is one of the most beautiful parts of France, not even its best friend could describe the terrain as easy. Even so, this seemed a good reason to attack the duty-frees again. Then we climbed back into the car and sped off down the mountain, on another of Geoff's white-knuckle specialities, into the valley of the Jonte.

Night was already falling as we drove down, off the Col de Perjuret to our night stop at the Hôtel Family in Meyrueis. When we arrived, the Hôtel Family was being enlarged by the simple process of removing the roof, building on another storey, then putting the roof back. We stood in the street and watched the builders for a while. It all looked extremely hazardous to me, rather like building a real-life house of cards and seeing how high you dare go before it all collapses. Meyrueis itself is an agreeable place with the remains of old walls and towers, and a pretty quay, the *Quai Sully*, to promenade on beside the rushing river, or rather rivers, which run through the town, for Meyrueis stands at the point where the Jonte is joined by the Béluzon, at the head of the Jonte gorges, which are less spectacular than those of the Tarn but no less beautiful.

Early next morning saw us back on the Col de Perjuret, where the balmy evening of the previous day had been exchanged for lowering skies, low temperatures and a shrieking wind. This was bad enough, but our main problem now was what to do with Geoff's car. In the original plan, the car should have been left at Aumont, but since we had it with us, and there is no easy way to and fro across the Cévennes as there was in the Sarthe, we had no option but to ferry it forward and, although this meant that Geoff had to retrace his steps at least once a day, the advantages of having transport when the daily stint was over more than made up for any inconvenience. But, as Geoff said frequently, I would say that, wouldn't I; he was the one who had to go back and fetch the car. After two days motoring from the Channel, Geoff felt in need of some exercise, so we left the car at the *col* and walked on together to Cabrillac, a village below Mont Aigoual. Buffeted all the way by the wind, we arrived there thoroughly chilled, and lumbered into a small café, where several of the locals were holding forth to all within earshot on the iniquities of the Parc National des Cévennes.

This Parc National des Cévennes is the largest national park in France, covering an area of some 82,000 hectares, though that is only the central core; around that lies a periphery of another 236,000 hectares. In total the park enfolds a vast area of France, covering roughly 500 square miles from Mende south to Le Vigan, and from Ste Enimie east to Les Vans. Within this zone, wildlife is conserved and rural activities restrained, while development is subject to severe controls and commercial activity discouraged. Much of this may be all for the good, but the local people find their liberties severely curtailed, notably their freedom to shoot and hunt, and they don't like it; '*Merde aux Parc*' is only the mildest of the roadside slogans. The Cévenoles are an independent lot who don't see why the Central Government, which has given them no help in the past, should restrict their liberties now. In spite of the chilly day, the atmosphere in the bar was heated.

On a fine day, little Cabrillac must be a pretty spot, a huddled hamlet of small houses and barns with just this one café and a *gîte d'étape* for the locals and visitors to gather in. As French cafés go, it was rustic and pleasant, a long, low room, with walls of undressed stone, the rafters hung about with hams. Given the chill winds outside, I could quite easily have stayed in there, but Geoff had to get back to the car for, having had my car broken into six times on visits to France over the past few years, I was uneasy about leaving our transport standing unguarded on the lonely mountain. Besides, I still had some distance to cover before our night-stop at L'Espérou, so we emerged to an instant battering from the rain, and set off in opposite directions.

My friend, Tom Vernon, the 'Fat Man on a Bicycle', had passed this way when crossing the Cévennes on his bicycle ride through France, and had given me much good advice about attacking these mountains. Much of what he said I had forgotten, especially Tom's wise counsel on avoiding the top of Mont Aigoual in times of high wind. Mont Aigoual is a high, forested mountain, whose bare summit is crowned by an observatory which looks like a castle and dates from 1887. On the previous evening I had noticed that those parts of the building which were not made of stone or concrete were held down with chains – and rightly so. The weather up there can be violent, with the winds reaching speeds of up to 150 mph. On this cold, grey morning, the winds were not quite at that record velocity, but were working on it. While Geoff turned back to collect the car at the *col*, I wove my way up the slope behind Cabrillac, into the shelter of the woods, then over the ridge and out onto the open hillside between the road and the radio masts on the summit of the mountain. Out there the wind was terrific – when I faced into it, I couldn't breathe. Crouching under the blast, I stumbled on a tussock of grass and was immediately blown off my feet, rolling down into a snow-filled gulley where, if I kept my head down, standing was just possible. While crouched in there, catching my breath, I saw a red helicopter come skimming up from the north and attempt to cross the crest towards the observatory. When it left the shelter of the valley the nose dipped suddenly, and the tail rotor swung high and wild as the helicopter was blown steadily backwards by the force of the wind. It eventually turned away, defeated, the rotors making a mournful 'wop-wop' sound as it flew away to the west.

It was the wildest morning of my journey. The wind made the walking hard work and it was very cold. I have wondered since why I did not do the sensible thing and simply beat a retreat off the mountain and try another way, but when you have gained height on foot in steep terrain, there is a natural reluctance to surrender any of that hard-won altitude. Besides, I needed to stick close to the GR60 if I was to find my way to L'Espérou. I also had a theory that if I could skirt the summit to the west and get below the crest, then the trees would take the full fetch of the wind and life would become more tolerable. Anyway, if I stayed in the snow gullies or crouched in the lee of the crest, I could, with difficulty, proceed, creeping round and up to where the GR60 turned off the summit, and then down on to a wide track which ran steeply through the woods towards the ski resort of Prat-Peirot. Once over the crest, sure enough, the wind abated, although it was still perishingly cold. The branches of the trees were flailing and groaning above my head. But at least I had the consolation of knowing that any branches likely to fall had probably done so by now, so I jogged a little to get warm. Soon I found myself passing the ski-lifts surrounding the tiny resort of Prat-Peirot.

Prat-Peirot was a ghost town, a little place of stressed concrete buildings, clanking ski-tows and flapping flags and posters, deserted now that the bulk of the snow had gone. This is one of the smaller ski resorts of France and, while Lioran and Super-Besse still had signs of life, Prat-Peirot had clearly shut up shop for the summer. From here the path led down to the Col de la Serreyrede, another significant point on my journey. This is the watershed where the waters of southern France divide, some flowing west into the Atlantic, others south towards the Mediterranean. From here it was only a little distance over the crest and then down into the resort of L'Espérou, from where the *Grande Draille* leads south and east towards Le Vigan. To gain a little distance for the next day, I followed the GR60 waymarks for about six and a half miles, staying on or near the road, before I decided that I had done enough for one day and sat down by the roadside to wait for Geoff and a lift back into L'Espérou. With his car as back-up, I could gain a little more distance each day, and was glad to do so. I had now been walking for more than a month, and after that tantalising glimpse of the sea, I wanted to press on to the finish.

On the other hand, it was pleasant to walk down this historic *draille*, following a path along which drovers had led their flocks and herds for generations. In parts of the Cévennes – notably over on Mont Lozère – the practice has not yet died out. I would have liked to have met a flock, jangling its way along this path as they did in days gone by, but although I followed the *Grande Draille* for more than a hundred miles, I met no sheep, nor goats, and very few walkers.

The Cévennes is a Protestant land. It has been so since the days of the Reformation and has suffered for it, especially in the century after the Revocation of the Edict of Nantes. The Protestants of the Cévennes – *the Cévenoles* – refused to give up either their rite or their country. Finding that their obedience and conversion was not to be obtained easily, the King tried other methods, most notably the *dragonade*. Troops of the King's dragoons were sent into the villages, billeted on the local people,

197

and encouraged to do their worst. Their worst could vary from chasing the maids and putting their boots on the table, to all-out pillage and executions. But the *Cévenoles* resisted all persuasion and relentless persecution until 1702 when they rose up and killed a particularly persistent Catholic priest. The reprisals which followed this event led to the rebellion of the *Camisards,* the men in shirts, which was a full-scale civil war for two years, and spluttered on as a guerrilla campaign until 1789 when, with the outbreak of the Revolution, religious tolerance was re-established in France.

Fate, however, had other blows in store for the *Cévenoles.* The area had been famous for silk weaving, the hillsides around Le Vigan and Ganges once being covered with mulberry trees grown to feed the silkworms. The growth of synthetic fabrics killed the demand, however, and a series of great frosts killed off the trees, so little is left of an industry which once provided a reasonable livelihood for thousands of local people, and the land itself lies neglected. True, some farms still flourish, and the tinkle of sheep-bells is rarely out of your ears, but the terraces are crumbling, the narrow irrigation canals are cracked and dry, and the countryside is littered with abandoned hamlets or ruined *mas.* I must have walked through or around a hundred of these long abandoned farmhouses in my footpath journey across the Cévennes, and a sad sight they are. Further south, out on the Languedoc plain, vines cover the fields for mile after mile, adding their production each season to Europe's ever-spreading wine lake, but here in the hills the land is abandoned and reverting to the wild.

Come the dawn in L'Espérou, all was bright and fair. The terrain south is very rough and thickly wooded, and once I was out of the trees and on to the open ridges, the day turned very hot indeed. Of course I had forgotten to fill my water-bottle. Fortunately there is a *gîte d'étape* beside the *Grande Draille* an hour or so south of L'Espérou, where I was able to fill myself and my bottle with water, before plunging on again down the trail. This is jagged country, covered with dwarf oak, gorse and needlepines, but very beautiful in a stark fashion – especially on this morning, when the damp of the morning mist brought out the scents from the wild flowers, the honeysuckle and the lavender. As in every Eden, however, there were snags. The mountain paths are very narrow, rocky and uneven, hard on the feet, overhung by the dwarf oak and draped with spreading brambles and spinefex, a kind of thorny creeper that made regular grabs at my bootlaces. It was also very hot, especially up on the open ridge below the Col des Mourèzes. Moving fast, I was glad by midday to have cut the distance down and to descend to the road at Le Rey, limping along to Pont d'Hérault which, apart from being a cool spot, signalled my arrival in my last but one French *département*. I tumbled into the Hôtel Maurice at Pont d'Hérault where the owner insisted on bringing me several beers, *pour la force*, as the French often say, and refusing all payment, which is not quite so common – before crossing the river and climbing the far hillside for yet another ridge-walk, due south to Ganges. This path runs on the hill between the valley of the Hérault on one side and the valley of the Rieutord on the other.

The afternoon began gently enough, along tracks which led to more small, half-empty hamlets and more ruined, abandoned *mas*. As the afternoon wore on, though, and I became increasingly tired, the path began to climb up and up, rising relentlessly, and heading directly over Mont Méjean, a jagged mountain crest at the end of the ridge, standing a thousand feet or more above the valley floor. Then the path fell again, down over another lower crest, a hard, ankle-wrenching trail of piled rocks and slippery stones. It was rather like walking along the back of a dinosaur. Ganges was now in plain sight but getting no closer as the path rose and fell across the hills. I was often scrambling at this stage, using my hands to keep my balance over the rough ground.

I could well have done without this, quite the roughest walking I had met so far, because the sun was very hot and the air humid. The flies and midges became a pest but, worst of all, a great deal of effort seemed to give me very little return in progress made to the sea. It must be hidden somewhere in the haze ahead, that late-afternoon heat haze that now blanketed the vine-draped Languedoc plain below. Having accepted the fact that there comes a time on most days when there is nothing to do but bash on, I wiped the sweat from my face, lashed another thornbush aside with my stick, and forced myself up yet another sheer and rocky section of the path, ignoring my feet and the branches and brambles which tore at my clothing. I can't say it was fun though. It was early evening before I finally forced my way over the last ridge of this long mountain, coming into Ganges down a boulder-littered track that played havoc with my aching feet, arriving in the main street of the town just as an anxious Geoff was emerging from our hotel to look for me.

The Hôtel Aux Caves de l'Hérault in Ganges is a pleasant spot. Cool bedrooms, hot baths which are a comfort to tired limbs, and good food served on a wisteria-draped terrace, amid pollarded plane trees that look for all the world like vast candelabra, put an enjoyable end to a long and tiring day. We lingered out here until the other diners had gone to bed, chatting of this and that over a bottle or two of Listel. Next morning Ganges revealed itself as a very agreeable town with a huge weekly street market that kept us busy poking about the stalls until halfway through the morning, so it was already noon before I set out again, for St-Martin-de-Londres, hoping for a short and restful day.

Walking out of town down the road to Laroque provided a good start, for this little town stands beside the rushing Hérault river, and the restaurateurs were already setting their tables out on the *quai*, ready for the following May Day festivities. I kept on this road through the Hérault gorges as far as

St-Bauzille-de-Putois, from where I made my way back onto the GR60. Geoff, having already gone ahead to park the car and walk back towards me, appeared near La Cardonille with the good news that the countryside to the south soon fell away on to the flat, open *garrigue* and that he had already seen the high Pic de Loup mountain which rises up out of the *garrigue* close to the end of that day's stage at St-Martin-de-Londres . . . a doddle. He left me on the D1 road, in anticipation of seeing me at the farm of Lagarde in about an hour's time, and for about fifteen minutes I thought I would be there early.

After nearly five weeks' walking I should have learned that every day has its high and low spots and that so far this particular day was passing far too easily. The GR60 path rose and fell gently for a while, although it was crossing an increasing number of difficult, slippery stone runs. Then, quite suddenly, the GR60 path and the waymarks completely disappeared. I hunted around among the bushes for waymarks, failed to find them, and then sat down to consult the *topo-guide*. 'Here the path turns down The Chimney,' it said, 'and the walker must be prepared to be *"un peu sportif"* . . . for it may be necessary to use the hands.' Hmmn! With these clues, I found the GR60. It did indeed follow a chimney, a narrow gulley slashed down the cliff face, a sheer, 300-foot drop that I gingerly descended using feet, hands, elbows, knees and teeth ... these last for gritting. How anyone not more than a little *sportif* can get down that section of the GR60 in other than dry weather escapes me, for this gulley must be a waterfall when it rains. By the time I reached the bottom I was exhausted, trembling and drenched in sweat. All was not yet over, however, for I then had to descend two more of these *thalwegs*, a word I had never seen before, but which I take to mean 'gulley', and although neither was as steep as The Chimney, all took their toll of my remaining strength. It was a very tired old walker who emerged on to the edge of the sheer gorge of the River Lamalou, somewhere above the Grand Arc. I was by now very thirsty and eager, even anxious – all right, desperate – to get down to the river. But the path kept straight on halfway up the sheer cliff-side, with small stones slipping away into the void from under my now smooth boot-soles. By the time the path finally zig-zagged down to the river bed – which was as dry as any bone – I was completely exhausted.

I was also well on the way to heat exhaustion, my tongue swelling up nicely, but the path led on relentlessly, across the humped rocks of the dry river bed, climbed halfway up the far side of the gorge, and then down again to the river bed by the Grand Arc, a huge natural rock-arch carved in the walls of the gorge by the rushing waters of the river. When the river finally appeared as a series of stagnant pools, I was swaying on my feet, but thirsty as I was, drinking this evil-smelling, slime-coated, stagnant water was beyond me. I settled for soaking my neckerchief in the cooler depths below the surface and sucking that, before I turned away from the river to climb yet again up the steep rock-face to the top of the gorge. Forcing my way out of this thick and jumbled country at last, I emerged on to the main road at a point about two miles north of St-Martin-de-Londres, where an extremely anxious Geoff was on the point of calling for the *Gendarmerie de Montagne*. I had been missing for five hours, so his anxiety was understandable.

'Where the hell have you been?' he demanded, tearing the top off a can of beer. 'I've been waiting for hours. What took you so long?'

When I told him, he looked a little doubtful. He had already been down into the Grand Arc gorge to look for me, and an inspection of the map had failed to reveal how, apart from the terrain, I could have taken so long, or how we could have missed each other. As this had undoubtedly been the worst but also one of the most spectacular parts of the whole walk, Geoff decided that on the following day he would go in from the D1 to see it for himself, and that settled, I walked on into St-Martin-de-Londres, where we spent a pleasant hour resting in a café by the central fountain before returning to Ganges. I still had twenty-five miles to go, but tomorrow, with any luck, all this would be over.

May Day, *La Fête des Muguets*, the thirty-seventh day of my walk, began well when our hostess arrived at the breakfast table to present us both with bunches of *muguets* – lily of the valley – as is the custom in France on May Day. '*Ils portent bonheur,*' she said, and because happiness meant finishing this walk and sinking my feet into the Mediterranean as soon as possible, we pushed the coffee cups aside and studied the maps.

The shortest and therefore most direct route to the sea from St-Martin-de-Londres lay due south through Montpellier, a twenty-five-mile stage which would take me down to the sea at Palavas-les-Flots, on the western edge of the Camargue. This had a very definite appeal, for not only was it the shortest route and after 700 miles even a yard saved was a yard worth saving but the Camargue is a still-wild, romantic, very different part of France, full of fascinating places, and one which I wanted to see or rather, see again.

Many years ago, when I first came out of the Service, I took some time off to wander about Europe and catch up on my lost youth. Soldiering can be great fun but it does age you rather swiftly and you miss out on things. I completely missed the beginning of the Permissive Society, for example. I took a Bergan rucksack and my boots (soles-vulcanised), and set off to explore the real world, which was very different indeed back in the 1950s and, I suspect, rather nicer than it is today. Apart from a somewhat difficult time with the Spanish border guards at Hendaye, who finally stumbled upon my little currency racket and became very cross, I remember a time of sunshine, friendly people, improving French – and mosquitoes. I particularly remember the mosquitoes because the Languedoc coast behind the Golfe des Lions was infested with them, and they were particularly hellish in the Camargue delta, which lies between the two arms of the Rhône and Petit Rhône, and is the sort of marshy, brackish area where mosquitoes thrive. They must have been memorable, because thirty years later that mozzie-plagued walk still lives in my memory, along with the feeling that, in spite of their bites, the Camargue was worth it.

In those days tourism had not yet hit the Camargue – the mosquitoes saw to that. It was a place out of the past, where great herds of white horses galloped knee-deep through the swampy water, chasing herds of fierce black Camargue cattle, herded by the *guardiens*, the local cowboys. The *guardiens* look rather like the Spanish *vaquero*, with their wide-brimmed hats and high-cantled saddles, although they herd their cattle not with the *lariet*, but with a short, blunt-ended lance. Their beautiful white horses, which seem semi-aquatic and love the water, are supposedly descended from Arab horses brought here by the Saracens. If you want to see the *guardiens* displaying their skills and a most notable agility, the best way is to attend a *cours-libre*, or *à la cocarde*, the local version of a bullfight. In this, the bull is not killed, for the object is to remove a small rosette from between the horns while the bull, as bulls will, tries to flatten his tormentors against the nearest wall. I spent many afternoons sitting high on a fence, watching the local lads – the *razateurs* —dice with the bulls in the arena. And then there were the flamingoes, and the egrets; the chill, misty mornings, and the long, blood-red sunsets – yes, I had to go back to the Camargue.

I had been back since the 1950s, of course. Back in the 1970s I spent a summer in the Languedoc and wrote a book about it at a time when the whole coast was being developed. Teams of sprayers wiped out the mosquitoes – and nearly wiped out the flamingoes at the same time. Once one pest had gone, another one moved in – the developers – and today the Languedoc coast is studded with purpose-built resorts, Agde, Port-Bacarès, Port-Leucate, La Grande-Motte, and much of the old life has gone. However, here and there it lingers, especially out of season, and I have to admit that the absence of mosquitoes, or at least a decline in their numbers to a bearable level, is a definite bonus. There are places here that no Francophile should miss.

Chief of these for my money is the walled town of Aigues-Mortes to the east of Palavas, the City of the Dead-Waters, built in the thirteenth century by St Louis, the Crusader King, as his base for the Seventh Crusade. Some years previously, when Louis decided to fulfill a lifetime's vow and lead a General Passage to the Holy Land, he was faced with a major problem: he lacked a Mediterranean port to embark his army. The Crusader hosts had made themselves mightily unpopular on the land routes to the East, and it was both safer and quicker to go by sea. Louis purchased the site of Aigues-Mortes from the monks of Psalmodly, who scratched a small living here gathering sea-salt, but it was a fever-ridden spot and they were glad enough to give it up. Louis built the great Tower of Constance, which still glowers over the marshes and the channel, the *grau de Roi*, which connects Aigues-Mortes with the sea. He sailed for Egypt in 1248 with an army of fifteen thousand men, to be overwhelmed, defeated and captured at Damietta. It cost the French a fortune to get him back, but in 1270, when he was a very old man, he went crusading yet again, sailing from Aigues-Mortes to lay siege to Tunis. He died there, before the walls of that city, in the autumn of the same year.

Aigues-Mortes remained a considerable port, fortified by Louis' successors, Philip the Bold and Philip the Fair. Philip the Fair used the Tower of Constance to lock up the Templars when he purged the Order in 1314, and it remained a prison for centuries, finally containing *Camisard* hostages. One *Camisard* girl, Marie Durand, was put in the Tower at the age of eight, and kept there for forty years. When she was released in 1767, the bill stated that this was an act of clemency, not a pardon – no wonder the *Ancien Régime* fell. On an even darker note, Aigues-Mortes is said to be the port through which the Black Death entered Europe.

Today, or when I was last there ten years ago, Aigues-Mortes was attracting tourists and doing very nicely from the Yankee dollar, the flourishing trade in salt from the pans outside the walls, and as a centre for the Listel wines. I am particularly fond of the Listel *gris-de-gris*, a dry rosé. That was another incentive to finish this walk in the Camargue, where yet another attraction might be the coast that fascinated Van Gogh and Cézanne, and the gypsies' pilgrim centre of Stes-Maries-de-la-Mer. The gypsies believe that they came originally from Egypt – gypsy is said to be a corruption of the word 'Egyptian'. One gypsy legend has it that after the Crucifixion of Christ, Mary, mother of the apostles James and John, Mary Magdalen and Mary, the sister of Lazarus, fled from persecution in a boat. Mary Magdalen also brought her Egyptian servant Sarah, and the spot where they all landed here in the Camargue became and remains a pilgrim centre for the gypsies of Europe. They come here on 24 May each year for the feast day of Ste Sarah, their distant ancestor. They also come here to trade horses.

An alternative destination lay to the west. I could finish my journey at Sète, and that would not be a bad place either, for historic little Sète, the great wine port of the Languedoc, is a delightful spot, and one I thought Geoff would very much like to see. In addition they serve a hot fish pie there, a *tielle,* and the thought of ending my walk at a quayside table in Sète, with a well-chilled bottle of Listel *gris-de-gris* and a hot *tielle,* was almost irresistible. Why are there always these decisions?

Sète was built in the late seventeenth century by the orders of Louis XIV's chief minister, Colbert, as the country's chief Mediterranean port and the southern terminal of Paul Riquet's Canal du Midi, which was then nearing completion. When the port was opened in 1670, Colbert himself attended the celebrations, an event marked by the invention of a new dish –

Sole Colbert – and by a presentation of the now celebrated *joute,* or water-jousting, which is a sport that the fishermen of the littoral have enjoyed and practised from that day to this. The visitor stands a good chance of seeing this sport on any Sunday evening in summer, at any one of half a dozen harbours along the coast.

Two boats, one red, one blue, with flags and drummers, are rowed against each other by teams of oarsmen, while the jousters with lance and shield stand on high platforms at the stem, trying to pitch one another into the water. It's all great fun and I recall noting that when the lads of Sète came to fight the lads of Agde some years ago, they brought with them several lovely young ladies and twenty-five crates of beer. There are certain traditions though; the bachelors are always in the red boat, and the married men in the blue one, while the fishermen always joust under blue colours against land-based teams.

Sète is also the birthplace of the poet Paul Valéry, born there in 1871, and buried there in 1945. He wrote his greatest work, *Le Cimetière Marin,* about the cemetery just above the shore there, where he himself now lies, and just below that the townsfolk have built the *Théâtre de la Mer,* where his works are regularly performed. Throw in some fine restaurants, an abundance of seventeenth-century architecture, and recall that fishing ports are always fascinating, and it appeared that a finish at Sète might be no bad thing either. However, there remained Montpellier, which I could hardly miss.

Montpellier is the capital of the Languedoc and of the Hérault. A much modernised place, it is dominated today by the need to cope with the motor car, but it still has a lot to offer the history lover. In the thirteenth century it belonged to the short-lived Kingdom of Mallorca, which also comprised the Balearics and the County of Roussillon. The last King of Mallorca and Lord of Montpellier was killed by the English on the battlefield of Crécy in 1346. The University is medieval, and has a noted medical faculty where Rabelais studied between 1530 and 1538, and it was here that he wrote *Pantagruel* and *Gargantua*.

So, which way to go? Due south through Montpellier to Palavas and the Camargue, or angle west to Sète – or east, across the marshes, to Aigues-Mortes? All these places would make an attractive finish, but the western or eastern choices would require at least two more days on the trail. Besides, other writers had visited some of these places before. Tom Vernon had finished his ride at La Grande-Motte and Bernard Levin started in *Hannibal's Footsteps* from Aigues-Mortes. I asked Geoff what he thought.

'It's up to you, but the point you finish at hardly matters. This walk ends when you put your feet in the Mediterranean,' he pointed out. 'That's been the object of the entire exercise, and nothing else counts. If you go west you have this huge lake, the Etang de Thau, to get round, and an oil refinery to skirt. If you go east you have the A9 motorway to cross, then the Montpellier suburbs and maybe even the airport. It's up to you, but I should yomp it to the coast. It's only twenty-five miles and you can do it in a day if you put your mind to it.'

That seemed to settle it. May Day was as good a day as any on which to finish my walk, and after thirty-seven days tramping from Ouistreham and with 700 miles completed, I was anxious to get it done. I would head directly for Palavas while Geoff occupied himself in the wild country at our back, along the GR60 to the east of the Hérault.

'You just be careful in there,' I told him, as we packed up to leave. 'It's not as easy as you might think. If anything happens to me, you're my back-up, but if anything happens to you, it might be a day or more before I can get back and find you. I don't have any transport.'

That said, I set out across the *garrigue* for Palavas-les-Flots, and the end of my walk across France.

Looking back on this walk months after it was over, certain regions remain in my mind as offering the finest places for a walking holiday, places where I might want to return to again, or which I could recommend to others. However, on deeper reflection, I don't really know. When you walk right across a country, it all hangs together as a piece, and even the parts that were not exactly fun, still have a useful place in the memory. I think if you are going to do it at all, you should do the lot and take the rough with the smooth, the good with the bad.

However . . . if I must choose, then I must say that where to walk in France depends on the sort of walking you want. A browse through the hundred or so *topo-guides* at Stanfords or McCarta will reveal footpaths of every length and degree of difficulty. Dear Geoff had wisely chosen to direct my route through excellent walking areas; the Suisse-Normande, the Puy-de-Dôme, across that most glorious Cantal. I would not have missed those days on the *Sentier Haute-Auvergne* or down the *Tour des Monts de l'Aubrac* to Aumont, and if you – like me – love the open, soaring country, pack your boots right now and make for the Grandes Causses or the Puy-de-Dôme. For a challenge? Well, just keep on walking and it will become a challenge in the end. I suppose the GR4 from Besse to St Flour is a challenge, but a delightful one, and crossing the Cévennes can never be exactly easy; the heat and the terrain will see to that. But if I was asked where to go and pressed to recommend an area, these points apart, I would have very little to suggest. As we used to say in the Commandos, flogging along under our packs, it's all in the heart and the mind. Everyone must find their own far country in their own way. This walk was mine.

Two emotions conflict at the end of any journey. The first is a definite sense of relief that the whole exhausting thing will soon be finished and I can finally go home. The second is a slight sadness that yet another adventure is over. As I get older, this last feeling is increasingly tinged by the knowledge that I will never do anything like this again, that the sands of time are slowly but surely running out. Therefore this is also the time when I start wondering what I might do next. Walking across France is not a tremendous feat, for anyone can do it given the time, but on the other hand, not many have. It does require a certain amount of what I have heard described as 'stick-at-it-iveness'.

I had set out to walk from one coast to the other, following the footpaths and having a good time, and with the odd hiccup here and there I had done all that. By pushing on and exceeding my allotted distance, I had even covered the distance in five days fewer than originally planned, although that did not matter. It was not a race, and I only went further on some days because that place a few miles ahead looked a little more interesting than the place where I planned to stop. Perhaps it was all self-indulgence, but if so, I had paid a price for it in sweat and done no one any harm. All I had to do now, on this May-Day morning, was to reach my final destination, down at the far blue sea.

The *garrigue,* that low scrub and oak-tree country around St-Martin-de-Londres, is not the easiest terrain to cross. It's flat enough, though covered with small rocks and sharp stones, but pushing one's way through or under dusty dwarf oaks becomes very wearing after an hour or two. Fortunately there were little bars here and there to break up the morning and I made good time, at least to begin with. But then the day grew hotter and my pace slowed, so that it was mid-afternoon before I reached the outskirts of Montpellier, and four o'clock before Geoff, a dusty, sweaty, slightly wild-looking Geoff, came gliding to a halt alongside. I sat on a window-ledge, looking at him across the pavement, glad to rest my feet and sit in the shade for a moment.

'Well, how was it?' I asked. 'A piece of cake?'

'It was bloody awful,' said Geoff. 'Why didn't you warn me? I went on and on, up the path, into the gorge, and couldn't find the waymarks up the far side. It took hours to get to The Chimney

210

and then I nearly broke my neck on the climb up when a branch broke off in my hands. That's a typical French trick, to lead a path straight up a precipice. Anyway, how far is it now to the sea?'

'About six miles.'

'A doddle! Why don't we stop for a beer?'

For our beer we pressed on to the *Place de la Comédie,* the central square of Montpellier, which the students in this university town used to call *L'Oeuf* – the egg. *L'Oeuf* is rather splendid, wide, café-fringed – a place where people stroll about or sit and watch the strollers, or watch the water playing in the fountains – very restful on a hot afternoon. Montpellier is one of the finest of all the fine French provincial cities, but on this particular afternoon I simply wasn't in the mood for it. I wanted to finish this walk.

It might have been nice to end the walk on some airy peak, like stout Cortez, or by coming down a quiet path on to a deserted wave-washed beach, but life isn't like that. This crowded road between Palavas and Montpellier was a reminder that my peaceful footpath days were almost over. This was 'Welcome to the World' with a vengeance, and the world is all too often noisy, crowded and full of traffic. Even so, and in spite of the traffic, there were some definite compensations. Once off the road, the evening was still and warm, and white Camargue horses were wading in the reeds beside the road, one of them nursing a black foal. Camargue horses are born black, turning white later, and no animal is quite as delightful as a scampering foal. That was one diversion. Further out, in the shallow waters of the salt-flats, a large flock of pink flamingoes provided another by wading about and dipping their great beaks into the murky water in search of shrimps. It all helped to keep my mind off my feet as I wobbled across the bridge over the Rhône-Sète canal and finally found Geoff leaning on the Palavasles-Flots roadsign.

'I can spot that hobble of yours a mile off,' he said, grinning. 'But I'm proud of you . . . honestly. Seven hundred miles completed, and only about half a mile to go. Are you quite sure you don't want to stop?'

It seemed longer, but then the last bit always does. The sea stubbornly refused to come into sight, until I turned the last corner. Then, suddenly, there it was, wide and blue, running off to the far horizon, pounding hard on the sand, the curling wave-tops pink-tipped by the setting sun. I crossed the beach, reached the first rushing ripple, and kept on going, deeper into the water, until I was hip-deep in the sea with the undertow sucking the sand away beneath my boots.

'Will this do?' I asked Geoff. 'Have I definitely done it?'

'Yes, yes, yes,' said Geoff, putting away his camera. 'No one can say you haven't done it. Now come out and let's go and drink some Champagne.'

We splashed back across the sand, among scattered groups of families slowly packing up their things at the end of the day, and into a café just behind the beach. No one took the slightest notice of the wet Englishman with the heavy rucksack, but then the French are like that. Besides, it is well known that *Les Anglais sont foux*. It was all something of an anti-climax.

'So,' said Geoff at last, removing his beard from the glass. 'Now you've got that out of your system, what are we going to do next?'

'I'll think of something,' I said.

CLOTHING AND KIT LIST

The golden rule for any walking trip is the less you carry the better. The following list is what I started out with, but I shed as much as I could along the way and in the event many items turned out to be unnecessary – at least on my journey.

Clothing
1 pair Daisy Roots light boots
1 pair trainers
2 pairs Rohan 'Bags'
1 Rohan 'Pampas' jacket
1 pullover
2 pairs underpants
2 shirts
6 pairs loop-stitched socks
Handkerchiefs
Washing and shaving kit
First-aid kit
Beret, neckerchiefs, gloves
Set Berghaus 'Gore-Tex'
  rain-clothing
Set Yeti gaiters

Camping
1 Robert Saunders 'Jet-Packer'
  tent
1 self-inflating Thermarest
  mattress
1 Blacks 'Icelandic' sleeping bag
Torch, knife, hip-flask

Writing and Photography
2 notebooks
3 pens
2 x Nikon cameras
6 x rolls Ektachrome 100
  colour-slide film
6 x FP4 black & white film
Lenses and filters (various)

Maps and Guides
Topo-guides to GR 36
  (Ouistreham-Le Mans), GR41,
  GR60 *(Grande Draille)*, *Guide de
  Sentier de Haut-Auvergne, Sentier
  Tour des Monts de l'Aubrac*
Institut Géographique National
  IGN Maps:
  1:25,000, Monts de Cantal and
  1:100,000 Nos. 18, 19, 26, 34,
  35, 42, 49, 58, 65, 66 - Caen to
  Montpellier and Palavas-les-Flots
1 Silva compass

USEFUL ADDRESSES

The French Government
   Tourist Office,
178 Piccadilly,
London W1V OAL.
Tel: 01-491 7622.

Maps & Guides
McCarta Ltd,
122 King's Cross Road,
London WC1.
Tel: 01-278 8276.

Edward Stanford Ltd,
12 Long Acre,
London WC2.
Tel: 01-836 1321.

Institut Géographique National
   (IGN),
107 rue La Boetie,
75008 Paris,
FRANCE

Organisations
Fédération Française de
   Randonnée Pédestre (FFRP),
8 avenue Marceau,
75008 Paris,
FRANCE.

Confraternity of St James (for
   the Road to Compostela),
c/o 57 Leopold Road,
London N2 8BG.
Tel: 01-883 4893.

Club Alpin Français,
9 rue La Boetie,
75008 Paris,
FRANCE.
Tel: (1) 47 42 38 46.

Fédération des Parcs Naturels
   de France,
4 rue de Stockholm,
75008 Paris,
FRANCE
Tel: (1) 42 94 90 84.

Fédération Unie des Auberges
   de la Jeunesse,
6 rue Mesnil,
75116 Paris, FRANCE
Tel: (1) 45 05 13 14.

Brittany Ferries,
The Brittany Centre,
Albert Johnson Quay,
Portsmouth PO2 7AE.
Tel: 0705 819416.

SELECT BIBLIOGRAPHY

Collins, Martin, *Visitor's Guide to Normandy*, Moorland, 1986.

Evans, Jon, *Abroad*, Gollancz, 1968.

Debidour, V.H., and Plessy, B., *L'Auvergne*, Arthaud, 1976.

Fussell, Paul, *Abroad*, Oxford University Press, 1981.

Guide Gault-Millau 1987, Gault-Millau.

Hunter, Rob, *Walking in France*, Oxford Illustrated Press, 1981.

Hunter, Rob, and Wickers, David, *Classic Walks in France*, Oxford Illustrated Press, 1985.

Michelin Green Guides:*Normandy* (1985).

Châteaux of the Loire (1985).

Berri-Limousin (1982).

Auvergne (1986).

Causses-Languedoc (1979).

Roberts, Nesta, *Companion Guide to Normandy*, Collins, 1980.

Stevenson, R.L., *Travels with a Donkey in the Cévennes*, Century, 1985.

Vernon, Tom, *Fat Man on a Bicycle*, Michael Joseph, 1981.

INDEX

Agincourt, Battle of 88, 110
Aigoual, Mont 26, 189, 190, 194, 195
Aigues-Mortes 27, 205, 206, 208
Albigensian (Crusade) 80
Alençon 57, 58, 59, 60, 62, 64
Allegre, Yves d' 123
Alleuze 159, 160
Allier, River 159, 160
Alpes-Mancelles 60, 61
Amboise 73, 74, 75
Ander, River 159
Anjou 73, 81, 83
Armorican Massif 41
Aubrac plateau 145, 167, 168, 169, 170, 175
Aubrac (village) 169, 170
Aubusson 26, 94
Aumont-Aubrac 167, 171, 172, 175, 209
Aurillac 144
Auvergnats 109, 111, 126, 127, 128, 166
Auvergne 22, 25, 26, 79, 88, 89, 95, 98, 107, 109, 112, 114, 115, 116-136
Auvray, La Forêt 47, 48
Auxillac 182
Avantigny 72
Aveyron 148
Azay-le-Rideau 73, 75
Azay-sur-Cher 77
Azay-sur-Indre 84

Baedeker, Dr 14
Balue, Cardinal 85
Balzac 66
Banson, Puy de 122
Beaulieu-les-Loches 84
Beaumont-sur-Sarthe 61, 63, 64, 67, 72
Beaune-le-Froid 129, 130
Béluzon 193

Bénouville 32, 34, 35
Berri 94, 98, 99
Berri, Jean Duc de 87, 88
Bertrand, General 95, 164
Bés, River 162, 167
Besse-en-Chandesse 129
Besse-St-Anastaise 132
Bessols 160
Blois, Counts of 81
Borgia, Cesare 123
Bourg St Marc 46
Bourges 88
Boussac 101, 102, 103, 113
Bovines, Battle of 69
Brenne 93
Brittany 15
Burgundy, Dukes of 85, 87
burons 143, 149, 177
Butler, Samuel 152
Butte de Chaumont 58
Buzançais 90, 91, 93

Cabrillac 194, 195
Caen 16, 18, 25, 32, 34, 36, 37, 38, 59, 120
Calvados 33, 54
Camargue 203, 204-206, 211
Camerone 69
Cantal 26, 108, 112, 113, 114, 125, 126, 130, 136, 137-156, 209
Capets 81
Carrouges 53, 55, 56
Causse de Sauveterre 180, 181, 183, 185, 189
Causse Méjean 181, 188, 189
Cévennes 22, 26, 41, 181, 189, 191, 193-212
Chaîne des Dômes 115

Chambon-sur-Lac 129, 130
CHAMINA 157
Chamberboux 183, 184, 185
Chanac 183
Chancelade 108, 112, 113
Charles VI 88
Charles VII 75, 85, 186
Charles VIII 74, 75
Châteauroux 26, 50, 83, 88, 93, 94, 97
    Forêt de 95, 97
Château-sur-Cher 107
Châtillon-sur-Indre 88, 188
Chaumiane 134
Chemin de St Jacques 170
Chenonceau 73, 74
Cher, River 25, 73, 74, 108
Chilkoot Pass 12
Chirac 180
Clécy 45, 60
Clermont-Ferrand 124, 125, 126
Colbert 206
Col de Perjuret 189, 193, 194
Combrailles 107
Commandos, Royal Marines 59, 126,182
Compains 134
Condat 140
Cordes, Château de 122, 123, 124
Cormery 76, 77, 81, 83
Cotentin (peninsula) 32, 45
Couffinet 176
Courbepeyre 167, 168
Creuse, River 88, 99, 102
Creux de Soucy 133

D-Day 17
Dienne 142
Drouille, Forêt de 108

Egliseneuve-d'Entraigues 135, 136, 137,
    139, 140
Esclauze, Lac de l' 140
Espinat 134, 135
Estrées 90
Evaux-les-Bains 26, 106, 107

Fau-de-Peyre 168

Fayette, Maquis de la 84
Fédération pour la Randonnée Pédestre
    (FFRP) 13, 39, 44
Florac 41
Fossel, Theo 105, 106
Fournels 167
Fournier, Alain 88
François I 74, 75
Fridefont 161, 162
Fussell, Paul 20
Fyé 62

Ganges 199, 200, 203
Garabit 159
Garban Bernard de 160
garrigue 210
Gazy 182
Gelles 114, 115, 116, 119, 121, 122, 128
Gévaudan 22, 26, 162, 164
    Beast of the 164-166, 168
Giraudoux, Jean 102
gîta d'étape 13, 15
Goshalk, Bishop 147
Goupillières 41
Grand Arc 175, 202
Grande Draille d'Aubrac 183, 189
Grande Draille du Languedoc 26, 181, 189
*Grande Randonnée (GR), Comité National
    des Sentiers de la (CNSGR)* 13, 15, 18
Grandes Causses 26, 181, 209
GR4 26, 94, 107, 112, 114, 122, 123, 128,
    133, 134, 135, 140, 141, 143, 144, 145,
    148, 150, 209
GR22 45, 60
GR30 131, 132, 133, 136, 140
GR33 122
GR36 17, 25, 34, 41, 46, 47, 48, 49, 53,
    54, 57, 58, 60, 67, 68, 83
GR41 26, 103, 107, 112, 113, 114, 122,
    123, 124
GR41-460, 104, 107, 108, 112, 113, 128,
    133, 134
GR44 185
GR46 25, 26, 83, 84, 87, 95, 97, 100, 101,
    102

GR60 26, 27, 176, 180, 181, 182, 185, 196, 197, 201, 208
GR65 170, 175
GR441 112, 129
Grandval 159, 161
Grisols 160
Guéry, Lac de 128
Guescelin, Bertrand du 101, 178

Henri II 74
Henri III 178
Henri IV 178, 179
Henry II 82
Henry V 88
Henry VI 88
Hérault, River 199, 200, 208
Hérouville-St-Clair 35
Hibbert, Christopher 110

Indre, River 73, 75, 83, 87, 88, 95
Institut Géographique National (IGN) maps 13

Joan of Arc 86, 88, 103
Jonte, River 193, 194
Joyeuse, Duc de 179

La Barge 160, 161
La Bastide 161, 162
La Bouay 132
La Cardonille 201
La Carrière du Monteil 141
La Chartre-sur-le-Loir 61, 69, 70
La Châtre 26, 95, 97, 99, 100, 101
La Chaze-de-Peyre 175
La Jugie 114
La Lande 46
Lamalou, River 201
La Marche 103
Languedoc 63, 80, 206
La Roche-Mabile 58
Laroque 200
La Route 63
Laurière 114
Laval 177
Lavaufranche 103, 104

Lebas, Monsieur 127
Leclerc, General 53
Le Cros Bas 183
Le Gué-des-Prés 72
Le Mans 61, 65, 67, 68, 69, 70, 71
Le Monastier 12, 180
Le Mont-Dore 26, 89, 112
Le Monteil 142
Le Petit Jolon 140
Le Poinçonnet 97
Le Puy 73
Le Tranger 90
Les Ancizes-Comps 112
Les Betz 115
Les Dejets 114
Les Monts 114
L'Espérou 195, 196, 198
Les Vans 194
Le Vigan 194, 197, 198
Limoges 102
Limousin 26, 83, 88, 95, 102, 103, 104
Lioran 140, 142, 143, 146, 147, 148, 197
Liozargues 150
Loches 84, 85, 86
Logis de France 15
Loir, River 70
Loire, River 17, 21, 34, 54, 73, 80, 81, 88
Lot, River 169, 180, 181
Lougé-sur-Maire 54, 55
Louis XI 85
Louis XII 74
Louis XIII 97, 179
Louis XIV 179, 206
Lozère 162, 197

Maine, River 57
Maquis 98, 120
Margeride 148, 159, 160
Marvejols 168, 176, 177, 178, 179, 180
Mas St-Chély 189
Massif Central 18, 26, 89, 95, 99, 104, 111, 114, 116-136, 181
Maurines 162
Mayenne (Maine) 56, 61, 69
May-sur-Orne 37, 38, 39, 40
Medici, Catherine de 74

Mediterranean, 12, 18, 26 *et passim*
Méjean, Causse 181, 188
    Mont 199
Melusine 82
Mende 187, 188, 189, 194
Ménil-Hermei 48
Mers-sur-Indre 98
Meyrueis 193
Millevaches 103
Miremont 112, 113, 114
Monges 122
Montcineyre, Lac de 134
Mont des Avaloirs 60
Montfermy 112
Montgivray 100
Montipouret 98
Montluçon 88
Mont Mouchet 105
Montpellier 17, 203, 207, 208, 211
Mont-St-Michel 15
Monts Dômes 117, 125
Monts Dore 114, 117, 128, 130
Monts du Cantal 26, 117, 140, 144
Multonne, Forêt de 60
Murol 129, 131

Nasbinals 169, 171
Nerra, Fulk 84, 90
Neuvy-le-Roi 72
Niherne 94
Nîmes-le-Vieux Roches 189
Nivoliers 189
Nohant 99, 100
Nozières 142, 168

Orcival 26, 114, 119, 122, 124, 128, 129
Orne, River 25, 32, 34, 40, 45
Ouistreham 16, 17, 18, 20, 25, 31, 34,
    38, 119

Pain de Sucre 45
Palavas-les-Flots 203, 205, 208, 211
Pallau 90
Pampeluze, River 108
Parc des Volcans d'Auvergne 125
Parc National des Cévennes 194

Parc Nomandie-Maine 25, 56, 57
Pavin, Lac 133
Pegasus Bridge 34, 35
Pellefort 114
Perseigne, Forêt de 60
Petit Rhône, River 177
Petite-Creuse, River 103
Peyre 168
Pic de Loup 201
Plantagenets 81, 83, 87
Plomb du Cantal 137, 143, 148, 150,
    177, 187
Poitiers, Diane de 74
Pontaumur 114
Pont d'Hérault 199
Pont-d'Ouilly 45, 46, 47
Pont du Bouchet 112
Pontgibaud 114
Prat de Bouc 148, 149, 150
Prat, Monsieur 135
Prat-Pierot 196
Putanges-Pont-Ecrepin 17, 26, 27, 41,
    50, 53
Puy de Banson 122
Puy de Dôme (mountain) 107, 112, 125,
    130
    (département) 26, 114, 119, 125, 136, 209
Puy de Montcineyre 133
Puy de Niermont 150
Puy de Sancy 26, 115, 117, 124, 125,
    128, 129, 130, 133
Puy de Seycheuse 143
Puy du Rocher 148
Puy Mary 144, 148
Pyrenees 14, 34

Rechin, Fulk 90
Reignac 84
Rhue, River 137, 139
Richard 'Coeur de Lion' 85
Richelieu, Cardinal 97, 179
Rieutord, River 199
Rimeize, River 168
Rioux 122
Roc de Peyre 168, 176, 179
Roche d'Oêtre 46, 47, 48

Roche du Bec de l'Aigle 143
Roche Tuilière 128
Roffiac 150, 151
Roscoff 16
Rouergue 148
Rouvrou, River 46, 47
Rouziers-de-Touraine 72

St-André-sur-Orne 37
St Aubert 48
St-Bauzille-de-Putois 201
St-Bonnet-de-Condat 141
Ste-Colombe-de-Peyre 168, 175
St Denis 60
Ste Enimie 176, 185, 186, 187, 188, 194
St Flour 25, 26, 94, 140, 145, 147, 150,
    151, 153, 154, 155, 157, 161, 209
St-Genou 90
St-Germain-en-Sarthe 63
St-Hippolyte 87
Ste-Jamme-sur-Sarthe 66
St-Jean-du-Gard 12
St-Jean-du-Grais 77
St John, Knights of 90
St-Juéry 26, 159, 162, 163, 164, 165
St-Léger-de-Peyre 168, 178
St Malo 16
Stes-Maries-de-la-Mer 206
St-Mars-d'Outille 69
St-Martin-de-Londres 26, 27, 200, 201,
    202, 203, 210
St-Maurice-près-Pionsat 108
St Nectaire 126, 131
St-Pierre-Roche 122
Ste Sévère 101

Sand, George 95, 99, 101
Santoire, River 140
Sarthe, River 54, 59, 63
Sauveterre (village) 185
Ségur-les-Villas 141
Sentier des Volcans d'Auvergne 112, 122
Sentier du Haute Auvergne 26, 157, 209
Sentier du Triangle des Combrailles 107
Sentier Tour des Monts de l'Aubrac 26, 157,
    167, 168, 176, 209

Servières, Lac de 129, 130
Sète 10, 25, 206, 207, 208
Sforza, Ludovico 86
Sioule, River 112
Sioulet, River 113, 114, 124
Sorel, Agnes 86
Stevenson, Robert Louis 12, 17, 23, 41,
    188
Suger, Archbishop 55
Suisse-Normande 17, 25, 37, 38, 40, 45,
    46, 50, 51, 209

Tarn, River and Gorges 26, 176,
    185-186, 188
Tati, Jacques 101
Ternes 167
Ternes, River 160, 161
Theroux, Paul 15
Thury-Harcourt 41, 43, 44, 45
topo-guides 13, 14, 19 et passim
Toulouse 80
Touraine 72, 73, 74, 81, 82, 83
Tours 25, 61, 69, 72, 73
Tracros 116
Tréviers 27
Truc de l'Homme 167-168
Truyère 159-162

Valéry, Paul 207
Vallée d'Enfer 177
Varennes 130
Vassivèire 125, 132
Vélay 12
Vercingetorix 124
Vergheas 108
Vey 45
Vienne 73
Villedieu-sur-Indre 94
Vivoin 64

William The Conqueror 17